Christ's Kids Create!
102 Favorite Crafts for Kids
4 to 14

By Deborah Stroh

Compiled and Illustrated by Deborah Stroh
Editor: Jane L. Fryar
Editorial Assistant: Beverly J. Stroup

Scripture quotations are from The Holy Bible: NEW INTERNATIONAL VERSION, © 1973, 1978, 1984 by the International Bible Society. Used by permission o
Zondervan Bible Publishers.

Copyright © 1992 Concordia Publishing House, 3558 South Jefferson Avenue, St. Louis, MO 63118-3968.

All rights reserved. Except for classroom use, or use in parish education programs, no part of this publication may be reproduced, stored in a retrieval system, or tra
any form or by any means, electronic, mechanical, photocopying, recording, or otherwise, without the prior written permission of Concordia Publishing House.

Write to Library for the Blind, 1333 S. Kirkwood Road, St. Louis, MO 63122-7295, to obtain *Christ's Kids Create! 102 Favorite Crafts for Kids 4 to 14* in braille o
for the visually impaired.

© 1992 Concordia Pu

Contents •

© 1992 Concordia Publishing House

Introduction

One day I watched a young boy working very hard to construct an airplane. He used a hammer, nails, wood, and construction paper. The project was coming along nicely even though one wing was crooked and a little longer than the other. Soon a well-meaning teacher came along. She began to "help" the boy. She fixed the wing and nailed it in place. The plane looked great.

As the children were leaving class, the teacher handed the boy his airplane. The boy just looked up at the teacher and said, "That's not mine, it's yours. You made it."

Sometimes in our enthusiasm to help, we step over the line. We detract from the children's ability to create and to be creative. The success of a craft period cannot be measured by how "perfect" a particular project looks. You can most accurately measure your success as a craft leader by looking for the uniqueness of each project and by thinking about the discussion that has gone on during the process of creation.

Encourage the children to experiment and create, to make their own patterns and designs. Praise them often.

This book has been put together to give you, the teacher, ideas to help reinforce the Christian concepts and themes you have developed during each day's Bible study. Use these ideas as starting points. In many instances specific suggestions for materials and sizes have not been given. Use whatever resources and materials are available to you. Ask for donations—margarine tubs, wood blocks, ice cream spoons. Many times members of congregations are just waiting to be asked.

Many people have shared their favorite ideas to make this book possible. I would like to thank them all for their help: Sharon Marshall, Judy Weinrich, Brenda Stutz, Jeanean Belk, Robert Rikkels, Claudia Pautz, Marlise Nagel, Joan Pignataro, Ruth Shoumaker, Melissa Luth, Karen Hartman, Jennifer Boston, Samantha Schwab, and Les Stroh.

And a special thanks to my sister, Vicki Boston, for all the suggestions she made and all the time she spent helping me bring this project to completion.

Debbie Stroh

© 1992 Concordia Publishing House

A list of ideas for Creative Centers

● *Allow the children to explore and experiment with some of the following materials.*

Printing ● ● ● ● ● ● ● ● ● ● ● ●

on paper
   wood
   cardboard
with sponges
   vegetables
   fruits
   cookie cutters
   hands
   feet
   objects

Rubbings ● ● ● ● ● ● ● ● ●

use crayons
   pencils
   chalk
over sandpaper shapes
   cardboard shapes
   outside textures
   sidewalks
   bark
   brick
   stone
   wood
inside textures
   carpet
   chair seats
   walls
   tables
   fabric

Collages ● ● ● ● ● ● ● ●

anything cotton
   lace
   ribbon
   paper
   buttons
   shells
   sticks
   feathers
   spools
   leaves

gravel
rocks
sequins
sponges
wallpaper
sawdust

on anything

nuts
seeds
bark
bottle caps
gum wrappers
coffee grounds
confetti
corks
crepe paper
fabric
glitter
straw
tiles
wood scraps
yarn
noodles

Stitchery ● ● ● ● ● ● ● ● ● ● ●

use yarn
   ribbon
   beads
   string
   feathers
   twigs
on Styrofoam plates
   meat trays
   plastic mesh
   cardboard
   branches

Crayons ● ● ● ● ● ● ● ● ● ● ●

(remove the paper and break them)
on paper plates
   boxes
   cups

wood
sandpaper
various shapes
of paper

Use a warming tray, cover it with paper.
Draw a picture or design—try crayon resist—paint over your crayoned picture with watercolors

Tissue Paper ● ● ● ● ● ● ● ●

torn
cut
wadded
use starch
   watered-down glue
on paper
   waxed paper
   plates
   cups
   boxes

Chalk ● ● ● ● ● ● ● ● ● ● ●

on sandpaper
   wet, dry paper
   coffee filters
   paper towels
use water
   sugar water
   buttermilk

Paint ● ● ● ● ● ● ● ● ● ● ●

on anything
   with gelatin
   watercolors
   finger paint
   corn syrup with
   food coloring
Mix with sand
   cornmeal
   sawdust
   glue

Use brushes
   sticks
   cotton swabs
   marbles
   toothbrushes
   vegetable brushes
   feathers

Sculpture ● ● ● ● ● ● ● ● ● ●

use clay
   junk
   boxes
   wood
   Styrofoam
   toothpicks
   straws
with wood glue
   craft glue

Murals/Banners ● ● ● ● ● ● ● ●

on paper
   cardboard
   plastic
   felt
Use paint
   torn paper
   marking pens
   crayons
   collage materials

© 1992 Concordia Publishing House

Creation Banner

ziplock bags

Whatcha Need

7 small, good-quality ziplock bags (sandwich size)
Construction paper
Glue
Objects from nature (seeds, sand, sticks, leaves, shells, etc.)
A photo of yourself
Water
Electricians' tape
Dowel, 8"
Yarn, 12" long

What different

things can you find in God's creation?

Whatcha Do

1. Bag 1: Using construction paper, cut or tear out letters to say "God made _____." Arrange them inside the bag and glue them in place.
2. Bags 2–6: Arrange individual objects from nature and the photo of yourself in these bags. Objects may differ depending on where you live. (Optional: Glue objects to construction paper cut to fit inside each bag.)
3. Bag 7: Pour approximately 1 cup of water into the bag and seal it.
4. Tape the seven bags to one another, front and back, to make a long banner.
5. Fold the top of the first bag over the dowel and tape it in place. Attach the yarn to the ends of the dowel to hang your creation banner.

Note: Objects need not be in any particular order. This is a touching-feeling banner to help children visualize the greatness of God's creation.

© 1992 Concordia Publishing House

WHATCHA NEED

....

Paper or sew-in interfacing,
one long narrow strip
Scissors
Dowel stick
Glue
Glitter
Waxed paper
(if you use interfacing)
Colored marking pens
Ribbon

Holiday Acrostic Banner

Make slits in the top of the banner. Weave the dowel through...

EASTER
Easter time.
A new beginning!
Sunrise Resurrection!
Time to rejoice!
Everafter
Risen is our Lord!

WHATCHA DO

....

1. Choose a word that relates to the lesson of the day (e.g., Easter, Christmas, Jesus, Savior).
2. Fold the top of the banner over approximately 1–1/2".
3. Cut six slits in the top and then unfold the banner.
4. Weave the dowel through the slits.
5. Using the glue and glitter, write the letters of the chosen word down the left side of the banner. Allow the glue to dry. (If you use interfacing, place waxed paper over your work surface.)
6. Help the children develop a story, poem, or individual words or phrases that relate to the word.
7. Let them use marking pens to write their thoughts on their banners. (Help younger students write and spell as necessary.)
8. Tie long flowing ribbons on the right side of the banner.

© 1992 Concordia Publishing House

Printed Banner

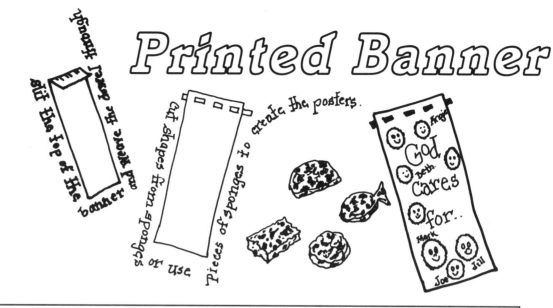

Whatcha Need

Old newspapers
Tightly woven material (burlap, felt, or vinyl)
Pinking shears
Dowel
Tempera paints
Liquid detergent
Marking pens
Paintbrushes
Sponges *
Yarn

Whatcha Do

1. Cover your work surface with old newspapers.
2. Cut the fabric banner background with pinking shears to the desired size. (9" x 18" makes a good sized individual banner.)
3. Turn over the top 2" of the banner. Cut slits into the fabric along the fold across the top.
4. Unfold the fabric and weave the dowel through the slits you just cut.
5. Mix 1 part detergent with 3 parts paint.
6. Use marking pens, paints, or letter-shaped sponges to print a Christian message on the banner.
7. Complete the banner, using sponges to paint designs.
8. Attach yarn to the ends of the dowel to hang the banner.
* Cut the sponges into the shapes you want or buy inexpensive shapes from a craft store.

Possible Themes:
Creation —"And It Was Good." *(Use cookie cutters as patterns on the sponges.)*
Noah's Ark—ark and rainbow. *(Use pieces of sponge to paint ark and rainbow. Trace around animal cookie cutters on the sponges. Cut out shapes.)*
"Gifts from God." *(Cut sponges into shapes to represent gifts: love-heart; food—apple; everlasting life—butterfly; friends and/or family—circles with smiles; forgiveness—a cross.)*

7

© 1992 Concordia Publishing House

Baptismal Banner

Whatcha Need

Tightly woven fabric
   (felt or burlap) 12" x 18"
Pinking sheers
Fabric paint with brushes
   or in writing tubes
15" dowel
Ribbon

Whatcha Do

1. Use pinking shears to cut the fabric into three strips: one 2" wide, one 6" wide, and one 4" wide. All should be 18" long.

2. Encourage the children to paint designs on their own banner using these guidelines:

On the 2" strip —their own name

On the 6" strip —Baptismal symbols

On the 4" strip —the words "I am God's child" or "You are Mine"

3. After the paint has dried, fold 2" of fabric over at the top of each strip and cut three to five slits. Unfold.

4. Weave the dowel through these strips, leaving approximately 1" between each strip.

5. Add ribbons to the ends of the dowel for decoration.

6. Tie yarn or ribbon to each end of the dowel to make a hanger.

© 1992 Concordia Publishing House

"Create a New Light" Window Banner*

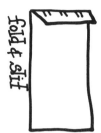

Whatcha Need

Broadcloth or any tightly-woven white material (hemming is unnecessary—the paint will prevent unraveling)

Fabric cutting board (cardboard)

Plastic wrap to cover the cutting board (to protect it from paint)

Straight pins

Pencils

Yard stick

A variety of fabric paints, including black

Paintbrushes

Wide-tipped permanent black marking pen

Café curtain hooks (*optional*)

2 suspension-style curtain rods (*optional*)

Scissors (*optional*)

A dowel, 1" or so longer than the width of the banner (*optional*)

Yarn (*optional*)

Whatcha Do

Note: Fabric paints are permanent! Have the students wear old clothes or paint shirts as they work.

1. Use straight pins to anchor the cloth to the plastic-covered fabric cutting board.

2. Create a design on the fabric using templates cut from cardboard and/or free-hand symbols. Draw these designs on the fabric with a pencil.

3. Then use a yardstick as you pencil in straight lines as shown in the diagram.

4. Working from the center outward, paint the design.

5. After the paint is dry, use a wide-tipped, permanent black marking pen or black fabric paint to paint all the lines to create a stained-glass effect.

* This can be done as a class project. Place the finished banners in a school or church window. To do this, measure the window you will use and cut the fabric to fit it. Use café curtain hooks and suspension rods to hang the banner in the window. If you are doing smaller, individual banners, cut five or six slits across the top and weave a dowel through the slits. Attach yarn and hang.

© 1992 Concordia Publishing House

Window Shade Banner

Whatcha Need

- An old window shade
- Scissors
- Dowels (*optional*)
- Paints, marking pens, or fabric paints
- Yarn

Whatcha Do

❶ Use the whole shade to make one large class banner or cut it to make several smaller, individual banners.

❷ If you decide to use smaller pieces, fold the top over and put several slits in the fold.

❸ Unfold the shade and weave the dowel through the slits.

❹ Use paints, marking pens, or fabric paints to finish the banner.

❺ Attach yarn as a hanger.

Possible **T**heme:

"Unto Us a Child Is Born" (stable; Mary and Joseph; Baby Jesus; stars; shepherds; sheep)

© 1992 Concordia Publishing House

Scripture Alphabet Banner

Whatcha Need

Tagboard
Scissors
A Bible
Fine-tipped marking pens
12' of ribbon at least 1/2" wide
Craft glue
Dowel

Whatcha Do

1. Have students cut 26 3" shapes from the tagboard.
2. Divide the class into equal groups, giving each group an equal number of alphabet letters to work with. Each group is to find one Bible passage that begins with those letters of the alphabet.
3. Write one Bible passage on each 3" shape.
4. Glue the shapes on strips of ribbon.
5. Turn the top of each piece of ribbon over the dowel and glue in place.

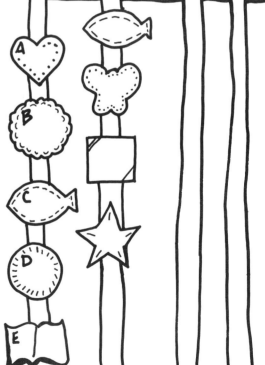

This activity is meant to be helpful in getting children into the Bible. Show them how to use a concordance to find key words. As children look for verses encourage them to find verses that have a message for them.

© 1992 Concordia Publishing House

Accordion Book

Whatcha Need

7 pieces of tagboard, all the same size and shape
Marking pens and crayons
Sunday school leaflets and magazine pictures (optional)
Glue stick (optional)
Stickers, scrap paper, and other collage materials (optional)
Hole punch
Yarn or ribbon

Whatcha Do

1. Plan, write, and illustrate a favorite Bible story on the pieces of tagboard. Draw your own illustrations, or use pictures from Sunday school leaflets and magazines.
2. Create a cover using marking pens and stickers, scrap paper, or other collage materials.
3. Punch three holes in the sides of the pages and the cover and use yarn or ribbon to lace these together.
4. Share your books with each other and take turns retelling the Bible stories.

Note: You could use these and other Bible stories: the creation; the Good Samaritan; Zacchaeus; Christmas; Easter; David and Jonathan.

Encourage the children to write the Bible story in their own words!

© 1992 Concordia Publishing House

Fabric Collage Greeting Cards

Whatcha Need

Construction paper
Fabric
Scissors
Glue
Ink pen or marking pen

Choose a favorite Bible

verse to write

inside the card.

Give the card to a friend or relative.

Whatcha Do

1. Fold a piece of construction paper in half.
2. Measure and cut fabric to the size of the construction paper card. Glue it in place.
3. Cut various shapes from other types of fabric and arrange them on the background. Glue these in place also.
4. Write a message or Bible verse inside of the card.

   Note: This card could be a cheery inspiration for a shut-in, someone who is ill, an invitation to Sunday school or VBS, or an expression of love to someone.

© 1992 Concordia Publishing House

Joy Cards

Whatcha Need •••••

- Construction paper
- Scissors
- Foil or cellophane paper
- Tape
- Marking pens (both fine-tipped and broad-tipped)
- Collage materials (e.g., rick-rack, small buttons, glitter, seeds)

Give or send cards to friends

Unto us a Child is born!

or relatives.

He is Risen!

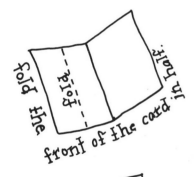

fold the front of the card in half

Cut out desired shape.

Jesus loves you

Tape foil or cellophane to the back of the shape.

Whatcha Do ••••••••••••••••••••••••••••

❶ Fold a piece of construction paper in half. Fold the front of the card in half again.

❷ Cut a shape out from the card's cover. Unfold the paper.

❸ Carefully tape foil or cellophane paper to the back of the cutout.

❹ Use marking pens to decorate the front of the card. Glue collage materials to the card, too.

❺ With the cutout shape as a pattern, use a fine-tipped marking pen to trace around the shape on the inside of the card. Do this several times, overlapping the shapes as shown.

❻ Use the broad-tipped marking pen to write a message and a Bible verse inside the card.

❼ Give the card away.

14

© 1992 Concordia Publishing House

Stained-Glass Candleholder

Tear or cut the tissue paper. Create new colors by overlapping the tissue.

Use your candle during family devotions.

Whatcha Need
- White glue
- Water
- Container for glue
- Paintbrush
- Clear, hard-plastic drinking glass
- Various colors of bright tissue paper
- Black permanent marking pen
- Baby food jar lid
- Votive candle

Whatcha Do

1. Mix enough water with the glue that you can spread it on with the paintbrush like paint.
2. Paint a small area of the drinking glass with glue.
3. Cover the glue with a torn piece of tissue.
4. Paint glue over the tissue and add more tissue.
5. Continue in this way until the glass has been covered with at least two layers of tissue paper. Then cover the whole glass with one more coat of glue. Allow it to dry.
6. Use a black permanent marking pen to add words that relate to the lesson (e.g., "Jesus, the Light of the World," "Jesus Is the Light").
7. Place the baby food jar lid in the bottom of the glass as a holder for the votive candle.
8. Insert the votive candle. Remind children that only adults should light the candle.

© 1992 Concordia Publishing House

"Shine Bright in His Light" Candleholder

Whatcha Need

Baby food jar ("beginner" size)
A roll of masking tape
Shoe polish (brown, blue, or burgundy)
A rag
Candle

candle

masking tape

shoe polish

Baby food Jar

small pieces of tape

Whatcha Do

1. Remove the label from the baby food jar.

2. Tear the masking tape into various sizes and shapes, each about 1/2"–1" in diameter. Stick these pieces onto the jar and smooth them down. Overlap the tape. Continue until you have covered the entire jar.

3. Use a rag to apply shoe polish in thin layers, first covering a small area of the jar with polish and then rubbing off the polish. This will create a mosaic affect. Let the polish dry.

4. Add a candle. The size of the candle determines whether you've just made a candle base or a candleholder.

Note: This small candleholder is ideal for use in a family devotion center. It will give the child who makes it "ownership" in the family worship center.

© 1992 Concordia Publishing House

Punched-Tin Candleholder

Whatcha Need

Empty pineapple cans
(without sharp edges) *

Water

Old towels

Hammer and nail

Votive candle

A hot pad or trivet

Tracing paper (optional)

Rubber bands

* Pineapple cans seldom have edges that will cut or scratch anyone.

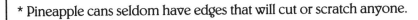

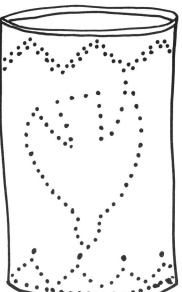

Whatcha Do

1. Fill the can with water and freeze it.
2. Remove the can from the freezer and place it on towels.
3. Use a hammer and nail to punch holes into the can.
4. Let the ice melt, dry the can, and add the candle.
5. Set the can on a hot pad or trivet before lighting the candle.

When the candle is lit don't touch the can—it may get hot!

Option: Create a pattern on tracing paper and use rubber bands to attach it to the frozen can. Punch holes along the lines on your design.

© 1992 Concordia Publishing House

Candy Creche
Group Project

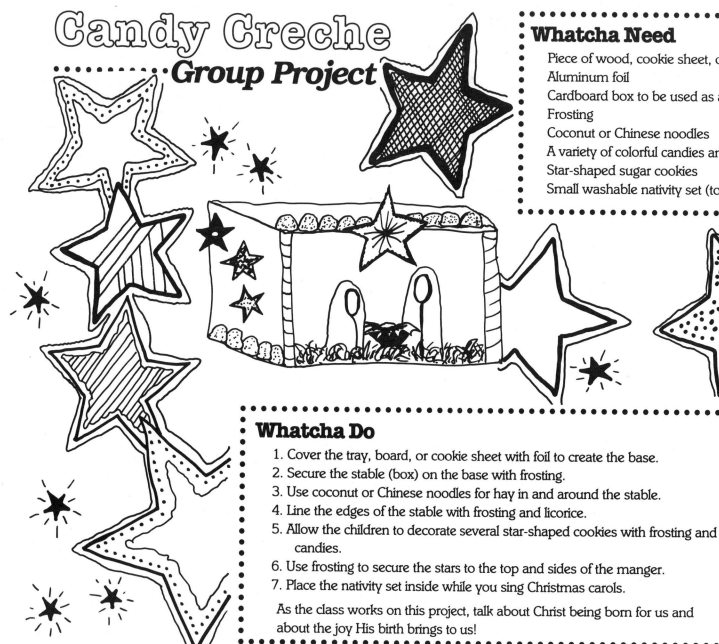

© 1992 Concordia Publishing House

Whatcha Need

Piece of wood, cookie sheet, or large tray
Aluminum foil
Cardboard box to be used as a stable
Frosting
Coconut or Chinese noodles
A variety of colorful candies and licorice
Star-shaped sugar cookies
Small washable nativity set (to fit inside the manger)

Whatcha Do

1. Cover the tray, board, or cookie sheet with foil to create the base.
2. Secure the stable (box) on the base with frosting.
3. Use coconut or Chinese noodles for hay in and around the stable.
4. Line the edges of the stable with frosting and licorice.
5. Allow the children to decorate several star-shaped cookies with frosting and candies.
6. Use frosting to secure the stars to the top and sides of the manger.
7. Place the nativity set inside while you sing Christmas carols.

As the class works on this project, talk about Christ being born for us and about the joy His birth brings to us!

Rainbow Cookie Creations

slice

curve on the cookie sheet.

Whatcha Need
Cookie dough
Flour
Food coloring
Rolling pin
Waxed paper
Cookie sheets
Cookie cutters (optional)

Encourage children to make their own creations.

Whatcha Do

1. Prepare your favorite roll-out cookie dough recipe or purchase prepared slice-and-bake cookie dough, adding enough flour so you can easily roll out the dough.

2. Divide the dough into five equal parts. Add one or more different colors of food coloring to each part (e.g., if you add red and blue, you will make purple).

3. Roll each set of dough into 4" strips, 1/4" thick. Stack these on top of each other, wrap them in waxed paper, and refrigerate them overnight.

4. The next day, arrange the slices of various colors appropriately, curve the slices into rainbow shapes and bake the cookies at 375 degrees for 6 – 8 minutes.

Talk about the promise God made to His people when He made the first rainbow or, as the children make their cookies, talk together about all the neat yellow (blue, red, green, purple) things God has created.

Option: Separate the different colors of dough and refrigerate it overnight. Give each child equal portions of colored dough, encouraging them to make their own creations. They can coil it, roll it into balls, lay pieces side-by-side or roll it out using the rolling pin. They may also wish to use favorite cookie cutters to create colored shapes.

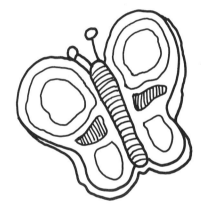

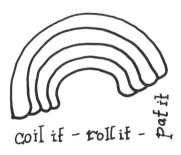

coil it – roll it – pat it

© 1992 Concordia Publishing House

Whatcha Need

- Cookie dough
- Rolling pin
- Cookie cutters
- Cookie sheet
- Craft sticks or dowels, 1/4" x 6"
- Icing (see recipe below)
- Plastic knives
- Cookie decorating candies
- Florist ribbon
- Permanent marking pen

Share a cookie pop with a friend.

Place a bouquet of cookies in a flower pot.

Jesus Loves You
Cookie Pops

A block of styrofoam helps to hold the cookies in place.

Whatcha Do

1. Prepare your favorite roll-out cookie dough recipe or purchase prepare slice-and-bake cookie dough. Roll out the dough to approximately 1/3"–1/2" thick.
2. Use cookie cutters to cut out shapes.
3. Place the cookies on a cookie sheet. Carefully insert the craft stick or dowel into the bottom of the cookie. Bake the cookies and cool them.
4. To make icing, mix 2 egg whites with enough powdered sugar to a stiff, spreadable consistency. Add a drop or two of food coloring. This icing will dry hard and is not very messy.
5. Ice each cookie pop. Decorate with candies.
6. Write a message, an invitation to attend VBS or Sunday school, or a Bible verse on the ribbon.
7. Attach the message to the craft stick on the cookie and give it away.

20

© 1992 Concordia Publishing House

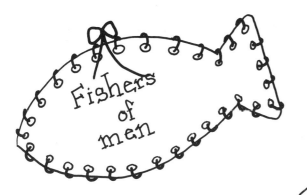

Whatcha Need

Patterns for crosses, butterflies, or hearts
Clear, plastic vinyl (found in most fabric stores)
Colored tagboard or a colored paper plate (optional)
Black permanent marking pen
Hole punch
Yarn or ribbon
Jellybeans or hard candies

Jellybean Shapes to Share

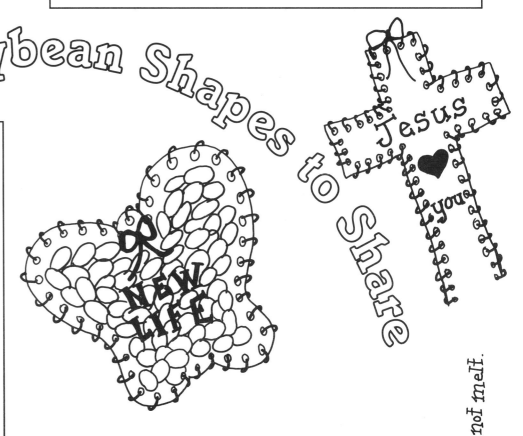

Use a variety of candy that will not melt.

Whatcha Do

1. Choose a shape to use from the patterns on pages 108 to 110. Use this pattern to cut out one vinyl and one tagboard piece to the desired shape. (You may use a colored paper plate instead of tagboard.)

2. Use the permanent marking pen to print a message such as "Jesus Loves You," "He Is Risen," or a favorite Bible passage on the vinyl.

3. Put the two shapes together and punch holes around the edge of the shape. (Make your holes no more than 1/4" apart.)

4. Use yarn or ribbon to stitch the two pieces together. Before you close the top, fill the shape with candies.

5. Repeat the process with a second shape. Give this one to a friend. As you do, tell that person about the message you printed on the shape.

Variation: Stitch two pieces of vinyl together to make a clear, plastic shape to share.

© 1992 Concordia Publishing House

Dough Picture Frames

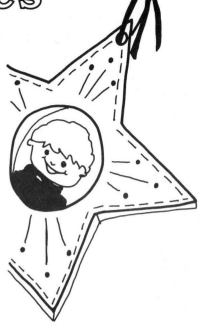

Whatcha Need

Dough, white and colored *
Rolling pin
Large cookie cutters (hearts, butterflies, etc.)
Foil-covered cookie sheet(s)
Round cookie cutter (one that will cut a circle small enough to fit inside the other cutters)

Toothpicks, forks, a garlic press
Water
Small paintbrush
Shellac or spray acrylic
A photo of each child
Glue
Ribbon

* Dough: Mix 2 c. flour, 1 c. salt, 1 c. warm water, and food coloring (optional). If the mixture is sticky, add more flour. If it's dry, add more water. Store in plastic bags until you are ready to use it. Bake creations at 250 degrees until hard (2 – 3 hours).

Whatcha Do

1. On a floured surface roll the dough to 1/2" thick.
2. Cut it into shapes, using the large cookie cutters.
3. Transfer each cutout to a foil-covered cookie sheet.
4. Use the small round cookie cutter to cut out the center of each shape. (This is where the child's photo will be placed.)
5. Decorate the dough frame using toothpicks, forks, dough pressed through a garlic press, and/or small pieces of additional dough. (When you add additional dough, paint the base with a very small amount of water. This will help it bond.)
6. Poke a hole at the top of the frame. (Later you will tie a ribbon through this hole to be used as a hanger.)
7. Bake the dough on a foil-covered cookie sheet at 250 degrees for 2–3 hours or until the dough hardens.
8. When it has cooled, coat it with shellac or spray acrylic. **(Be sure an adult does this in a well-ventilated area away from the children.)**
9. Glue the child's photo to the back of the dough frame.
10. Put ribbon through the hole at the top. Tie it in a bow and hang the picture on the wall or on a Christmas tree.

Options: Older children may wish to create their own frame shapes. Small mirrors may be used in place of the photo.

© 1992 Concordia Publishing House

Whatcha Need

Overhead transparency frames (available in many office supply stores)
Small pieces of sponge, feathers, cheap plastic combs
Tempera or acrylic paints

add lace – buttons – noodles – seeds – wallpaper – beads

feathers

sponges

paint

Whatcha Do

Simply dip the sponge, feather, or comb in paint and apply to the frame. (Squish the sponge, float the feather, and move the comb up and down on the frame.)
You can use a variety of colors and several techniques on the same frame.
Frame your favorite artwork.

Fun with Frames

© 1992 Concordia Publishing House

Whatcha Need

Picture frame, cut from cardboard or matte board
A variety of brightly-colored, thin yarn
Glue
Marking pens or puff paints
Picture (to be framed)
Tape
Cardboard or tagboard backing sheet (cut to the same size as picture frame)
Self-adhesive picture hanger

Yarn Picture Frames

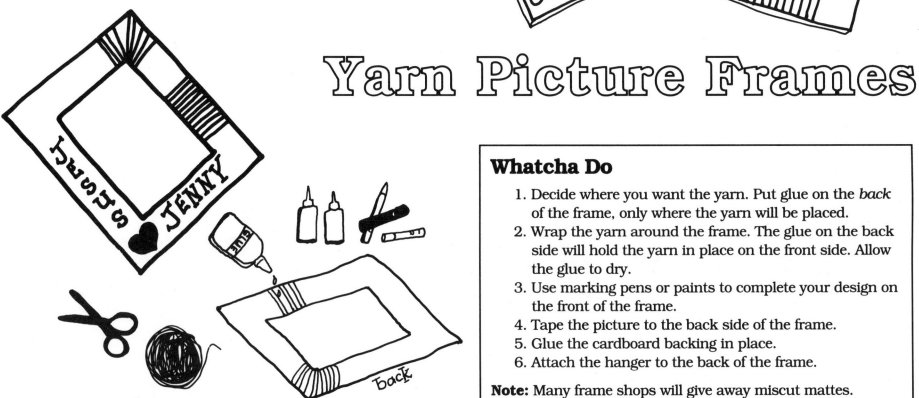

Whatcha Do

1. Decide where you want the yarn. Put glue on the *back* of the frame, only where the yarn will be placed.
2. Wrap the yarn around the frame. The glue on the back side will hold the yarn in place on the front side. Allow the glue to dry.
3. Use marking pens or paints to complete your design on the front of the frame.
4. Tape the picture to the back side of the frame.
5. Glue the cardboard backing in place.
6. Attach the hanger to the back of the frame.

Note: Many frame shops will give away miscut mattes.

© 1992 Concordia Publishing House

Glue Medallions

Whatcha Need

White glue
Food coloring
Cookie sheets
Waxed paper
Permanent marking pens
Hole punch
Yarn or shoestring

Whatcha Do

1. Add a few drops of food coloring to the glue in the bottle to achieve a desired color.

2. Squeeze the glue from the bottle onto a cookie sheet covered with waxed paper. The children may make a blob or attempt to make a symbol. (Note: The table or desktop on which they work must be even and flat.)

3. Allow the glue to dry 24–48 hours, depending on the humidity in your area.

4. When it's completely dry, peel the glue from the waxed paper.

5. Decorate your medallion with colored marking pens.

6. Punch a hole in the top of the medallion and string yarn or a shoestring through it so you can wear it as a necklace.

7. Make a second medallion to give to a friend.

Note: Precolored glue may also be purchased.

© 1992 Concordia Publishing House

Dough Jewelry

Whatcha Need

Dough *
Pencil
Cookie cutters
Foil-covered cookie sheet
Newspapers
Spray acrylic
Permanent marking pens
Paints and brushes (*optional*)
Long shoestring or yarn

* Dough

Mix 2 c. flour, 1/2 c. salt, and approximately 1/2 – 3/4 c. warm water. Knead until very smooth. You may wish to mix dry tempera paint with the flour and salt to make colored dough. Or put a drop or two of food coloring into the water before you mix in the flour. If the dough is crumbly add a little extra water. If it's too sticky, add more flour.

Whatcha Do

1. Roll small amounts of dough into balls.
2. Use a pencil to put a hole through each ball to make beads.
3. Take more dough and press it down flat. Use cookie cutters to cut shapes for the necklace. Put two holes in the top of each shape.
4. Place the beads and shapes on a foil-covered cookie sheet.
5. Bake them at 250 degrees for 1–2 hours or until they harden.
6. Place the beads and shapes on newspaper and spray with acrylic spray. **(An adult should do this outdoors and in an area away from the children!)**
7. Decorate the shapes with marking pens or paints.
8. String the beads and shapes on shoestrings or yarn.

© 1992 Concordia Publishing House

New Life Necklace

Whatcha Need • • • • • • • • • •

- 1 butterfly shape (*wooden or cardboard*)*
- 4 small hearts (*wooden cardboard*)*
- Marking pens
- Glitter
- Glue
- Shellac
- Yarn or shoestring
- 1 large, blunt needle
- Beads or small pieces of colorful soda straws

*All shapes need two holes near the top.

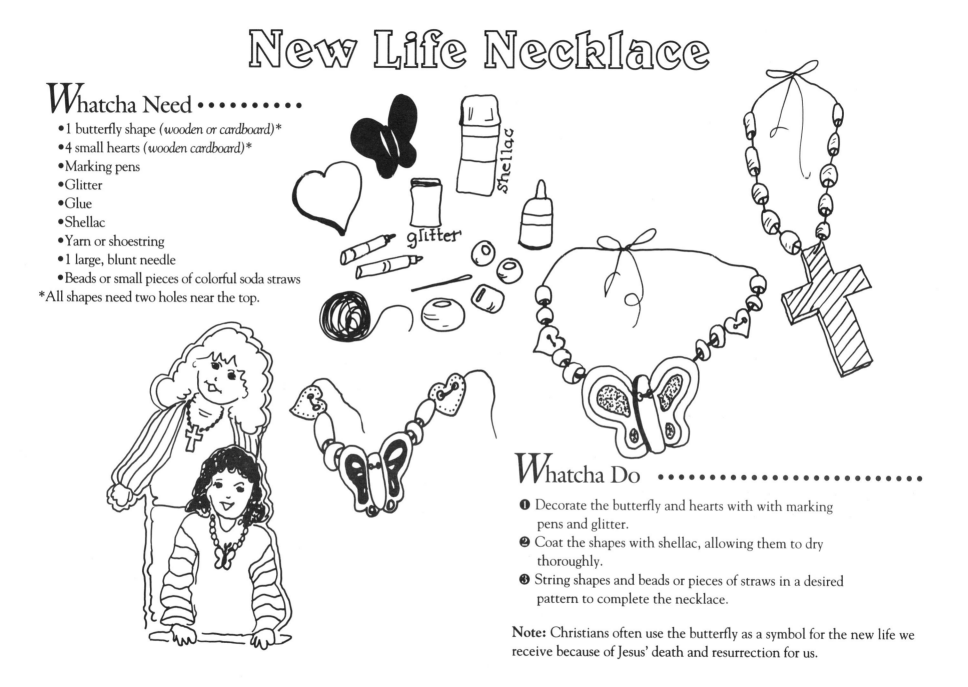

Whatcha Do •

❶ Decorate the butterfly and hearts with with marking pens and glitter.

❷ Coat the shapes with shellac, allowing them to dry thoroughly.

❸ String shapes and beads or pieces of straws in a desired pattern to complete the necklace.

Note: Christians often use the butterfly as a symbol for the new life we receive because of Jesus' death and resurrection for us.

© 1992 Concordia Publishing House

"Jesus Loves Me" Mobile

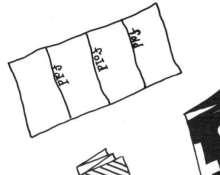

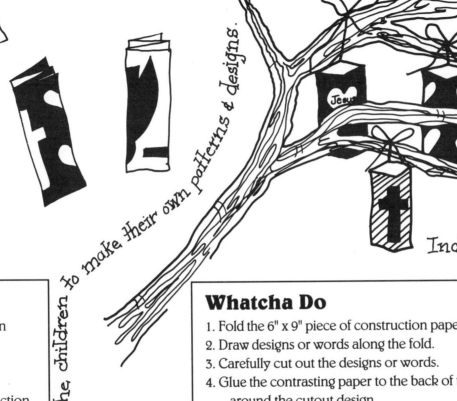

Encourage the children to make their own patterns & designs.

Include Bible verses on designs.

Whatcha Need

Brightly colored construction
   paper, 6" x 9"

Pencils

Scissors

Contrasting color of construction
   paper, foil, or cellophane
   paper, 5-1/2" x 8-1/2"

Glue or glue stick

Stapler

Hole punch

Ribbon or yarn

Small tree branch

Whatcha Do

1. Fold the 6" x 9" piece of construction paper in fourths.
2. Draw designs or words along the fold.
3. Carefully cut out the designs or words.
4. Glue the contrasting paper to the back of the cutout sheet. Glue carefully
   around the cutout design.
5. Form the paper into a long rectangular box (with the cutout design to the outside)
   and staple.
6. Punch two holes at the top. String the yarn or ribbon through the holes and tie the ends
   to the branch.

Suggested themes: "Jesus Loves Me"

The Trinity

Baptism

28

© 1992 Concordia Publishing House

Praise Mobile

Whatcha Need

A small tree branch

Items from nature (e.g., pinecones, nuts, seed pods, dried flowers, shells, drift wood)

Yarn or ribbon

A piece of tagboard decorated with the words "Praise God for His Creation" and a praise prayer.

Pictures of children (optional)

acrylic spray (optional)

Try seeds, nuts, shells, pine cones, leaves, drift wood, feathers, sticks, stones...

Whatcha Do

1. Take a nature walk to collect items for the mobile, including a small tree branch.
2. Tie a piece of ribbon to each object you find.
3. Suspend the branch from the ceiling.
4. Tie nature items to the tree branch. You may also want to add pictures of the children. Remember that the secret of a mobile is to keep everything in balance!
5. Work together to write a praise prayer and write it on the tagboard. Attach the tagboard to your mobile.
6. Spray the mobile with acrylic spray. **(An adult should do this in a well-ventilated area away from the students.)**

The Praise Mobile will look different in different localities. Help the class as they write their praise litany. Use a phrase of response as an echo throughout the prayer. See **Psalm 136** as an example of this kind of responsive prayer or litany.

© 1992 Concordia Publishing House

Whatcha Need

Butterfly patterns from p. 108 & 110

A sheet of acetate (e.g., the sheets sold for use with overhead projectors)

A variety of broad-tipped permanent marking pens

Scissors

Strip of tagboard or poster board, 2" x 18"

Stapler

A hole punch

Yarn or ribbon

"He Is Risen" Butterfly Mobile

Encourage the children to make their own designs.

Whatcha Do

1. Lay patterns for butterflies under the acetate.
2. Use a black marking pen to outline the butterflies. Work from top to bottom. (Do not touch the lines until they have dried, or they will smudge.)
3. After the lines have dried, cut out the butterflies.
4. Color the butterflies using permanent marking pens. Make each as colorful and bright as you can.
5. Print the message, "He Is Risen" on the strip of poster board and staple the ends together to form a circle. (Make sure students use the stapler with care; an adult should staple for younger children.)
6. Punch holes in the strip and use yarn to attach the butterflies to it. Add a hanger of yarn or ribbon at the top.

Variations: Use this process for any theme.

       Family: "Jesus loves _____"

       Put family members' names on hearts or drawings of the family.

       Creation: "God made . . ."

       Cut out pictures of the sun, moon, stars, flowers, animals, Adam and Eve.

© 1992 Concordia Publishing House

Whatcha Need

- Clear plastic tubing (available at craft, hardware, and aquarium supply stores), 1/2" in diameter
- Scissors
- Hot glue gun and glue
- Mineral oil or inexpensive baby oil
- Eye droppers
- Glitter in a variety of colors (at least four)
- Tagboard
- Clear fishing line
- Marking pens

Sparkle Rainbow

God always keeps His promises

Whatcha Do

1. Cut the tubing into four or five lengths. Note that each piece needs to be slightly larger than the last. Cut the first one, arc it, then arc the remaining tubing over it and cut it at the correct length for the second length of tubing, and so on. Cut as many arcs as you have colors of glitter.
2. Plug one end of each tube with glue from a hot glue gun. **(An adult should supervise this step closely!)**
3. Use an eye dropper to almost fill each tube with oil, one tube at a time. (Shake the tube gently as necessary to force out air bubbles.)
4. Add glitter and then more oil allowing for only one small air bubble in the tube.
5. Plug the second end of the tube with glue. Hold it upright until the glue dries. **(Again, adults must supervise use of the hot glue gun!)**
6. Repeat the process until you have filled and plugged all of the tubes.
7. Cut a piece of tagboard the length of your rainbow. The tagboard should be about 2" wide.
8. Glue the tubes onto the tagboard, creating the arcs of a rainbow.
9. When the glue dries, gently tie fishing line around the top of the rainbow as a hanger.
10. Print a Scripture verse or one of God's promises on the tagboard.

Option: Use small, colored beads in place of the oil and glitter.

© 1992 Concordia Publishing House

Joy Maker

Rejoice in the Lord

Sing joyfully to the Lord

Sing to the Lord a new song.

Whatcha Need

Contact paper, solid colored
Scissors
Plastic lid
Hole punch
Permanent marking pens
Jingle bells
Ribbon (curling ribbon works well)
Pipe cleaners (optional)
Stickers (optional)

Helpful Hint: Some bells have sharp edges and may cut through the ribbon. You may wish to use pipe cleaners to attach the bells. Then use ribbon to decorate the joy maker.

Whatcha Do

1. Cut the contact paper to fit the inside of the lid. Peel off the backing and carefully affix it to the lid.
2. Punch holes around the edges of the lid.
3. Using marking pens, write a message or Bible verse in the center of the lid.
4. Attach the jingle bells and, if necessary, extra ribbon to the holes.
5. Sing a song while making joyful sounds with your joy makers.

© 1992 Concordia Publishing House

JOY SHAKERS

Whatcha Need

Plastic or cardboard juice cans with lids
Dry beans or pebbles
Hot glue gun
Craft glue
Water
Paintbrush
Various colors of tissue paper
Clear acrylic spray

Parade through the school singing and praising God.

tissue

glue & water

Sing a new song

Whatcha Do

1. Put two tablespoons of dry beans or pebbles in the can.
2. Use a hot glue gun to fasten the lid in place. **An adult should do this.**
3. Mix one part water and two parts craft glue.
4. Paint a small area of the can with glue.
5. Cover the glue with a torn piece of tissue paper.
6. Paint glue over the tissue and add more tissue, until the can has been covered with at least two layers of tissue paper.
7. When the glue is completely dry, spray with a clear acrylic spray. **(An adult should do this in a well-ventilated area away from the students.)**

Children may use the Joy Shakers when praising God and singing songs.

© 1992 Concordia Publishing House

Nature Cross

Whatcha Need

Wooden or cardboard strips to form a cross
Wood glue
Sandpaper (*optional*)
Items from nature (small sticks, seeds, pebbles, pinecones,
   shells, etc.—whatever is easy to find in your area)
Picture hanger
Clear shellac or acrylic spray

Encourage the children to make their own crosses to help remind them of Jesus' greatest gift.

Jesus died for all!

Whatcha Do

1. Glue the strips of wood or cardboard together to form a cross. If you use wood, sand the edges.
2. Cover the cross with glue and arrange the nature items in a desired pattern. Work with only one section of the cross at a time.
3. Allow the glue to dry, then attach the hanger to the back of the cross.
4. Spray the cross with acrylic or dip it in shellac and let it dry. **(An adult should do this. Always work with shellac outside or in a well-ventilated area!)**

© 1992 Concordia Publishing House

Witness Rocks

Whatcha Need

Rocks (clean and smooth)
Acrylic paint
Paintbrushes
Permanent marking pens

Glue a few rocks together.

my
Jesus
friend

Jesus is the rock.

Jesus ♡ me.

Make an extra rock for a friend or yourself.

This is the day the Lord has made. Ps. 118:24

Trust in the Lord with all your heart.

Carry a small rock in your pocket.

Lead me to the rock that is higher than I... Ps. 61:2

Jesus

Whatcha Do

1. The rock must be clean and very dry. Paint a Christian symbol on the rock. (**Caution: Acrylic paints are not washable; they will stain clothing. Wear paint shirts or old clothes as you work.**)

2. Use a permanent marking pen to put a Bible verse on the rock.

3. As you give away each rock you have made, explain the symbol or Bible verse you have used in your design.

   Children may wish to make several rocks—one to keep and several to give away.

© 1992 Concordia Publishing House

Brick Bookends

Whatcha Need

- 2 bricks
- Paint (acrylic or craft)
- Paintbrush
- Sequins and glitter (*optional*)
- Shellac or spray acrylic
- Felt
- Glue

The Lord is my shepherd.

King of Kings

Therefore go and make disciples of all nations.

To us a Child is born!

He is not here. He has Risen

Whatcha Do

1. Clean the bricks and dry them thoroughly.
2. Paint pictures or designs on three sides of each brick.
3. Spray the brick with acrylic spray, or paint the brick with several coats of shellac. **(An adult should do this in a well-ventilated place, away from the children.)**
4. Glue a piece of felt to the bottom of the brick so it won't scratch furniture or the floor.

Decorate the bookends to go with any Biblical theme. Or use the decorated bricks as doorstops.

© 1992 Concordia Publishing House

Whatcha Need

- A shoebox lined with foil or plastic
- Sand to fill the box 3/4 full
- Spoon
- Rocks, buttons, sea shells, dried beans, costume jewelry (optional)
- Quick-setting plaster
- Paper clip

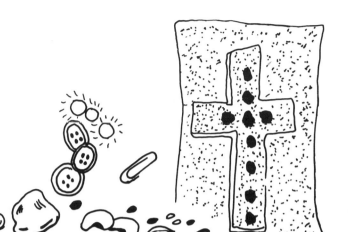

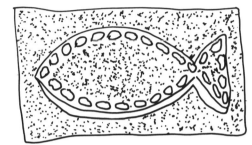

Jesus Christ, God's Son, Savior

shoe box

Plaster of Paris

foil foil foil foil

spoon

sand

Whatcha Do

1. Fill the box with damp sand approximately 4–5 inches deep.
2. Use a spoon or fingers to create a design in keeping with the theme of the lesson. The design should be approximately 2–3 inches deep. Add rocks, buttons, etc. if desired.
3. Mix the plaster according to directions on the package.
4. Pour the plaster into the box.
5. Hold the paper clip in place near the top of the figure until the plaster sets. This will make a hanger.
6. Allow the plaster to dry thoroughly.
7. Remove the plaster, brushing off the excess sand.

Sandcasting

© 1992 Concordia Publishing House

Bean Wreath

Whatcha Need

Paper doily or a piece of felt (larger than the tagboard circle)

Tagboard or cardboard circle (with a small circle cut out of the center)

Scissors

Craft glue

Lace or eyelet (optional)

Water

Assorted dry beans and seeds (in a variety of colors, shapes, and sizes)

Plastic spoon

Clear acrylic spray

Ribbon for bow and the hanging loop

If you are near a beach use very small shells.

Whatcha Do

1. Cut the center from the doily or felt and glue it to the back of the tagboard circle, or glue lace or eyelet around the outer edge.
2. Mix two parts glue with one part water.
3. Add assorted beans and seeds to the glue mixture and stir until well coated.
4. Spoon the bean and seed mixture onto the front of the tagboard circle, spreading it to the edges.
5. Allow this to dry overnight.
6. Spray with a clear acrylic spray. **(An adult should do this in an area away from the children!)** Allow it to dry according to the directions on the can.
7. Glue the bow and hanging loop in place.

Variation: Use this same procedure to make a cross or other Christian symbols appropriate for your lesson.

© 1992 Concordia Publishing House

Clay Plaques

Use with stories about creation - Baptism

- forgiveness - thanksgiving -

Whatcha Need

Self-hardening clay
22–32 gauge wire (approximately 2')
Waxed paper
Objects from nature (e.g., twigs, sticks,
    leaves, nuts, shells, rocks, evergreen sprigs)
Rolling pin
Pencil
Shoe polish (liquid or paste)
Soft cloth
Clear spray shellac or acrylic

Whatcha Do

1. Use wire to slice off a slab of clay, approximately 1/2" thick.
2. Place the clay on waxed paper.
3. Arrange objects from nature on the clay.
4. Place another sheet of waxed paper over the arrangement.
5. Roll a rolling pin over the waxed paper to press the objects into the clay.
6. Remove the waxed paper and the objects.
7. Use a pencil to drill a hole at the top of the clay slab.
8. Allow the clay to dry according to directions on the package.
9. Use shoe polish to color the plaque. Buff with a soft cloth. Work carefully so the clay doesn't break.
10. Spray the plaque with clear shellac or acrylic. **(An adult should do this in a well-ventilated area away from the children.)**

© 1992 Concordia Publishing House

Wooden Wall Hanging

Whatcha Need

Tree limbs, approximately 2" in diameter, sliced into 1/4" thick sections*

Sandpaper

Paint

Paintbrushes

Waxed paper

Hot glue gun or wood glue

Shellac or clear acrylic spray

Self-adhesive picture hanger or twine

* Perhaps someone in your congregation will cut the wood disks for you.

Encourage the children to create their own designs.

Whatcha Do

1. Lightly sand five wooden disks.
2. Paint one letter of the word J-E-S-U-S on each disk.
3. Arrange the letters vertically or horizontally on waxed paper.
4. Glue them together using the wood glue or a hot glue gun.
5. Shellac them or spray them with acrylic spray. **(An adult should do this outside and away from children.)**
6. When the disks are dry, attach the picture hanger or glue twine to the back of the center or top disk as a hanger.

Variations: *Use the words F-A-I-T-H or H-O-P-E instead of J-E-S-U-S. Or build a cross by overlapping the wooden sections.*

40

© 1992 Concordia Publishing House

Whatcha Need

Wooden blocks cut from 1" x 2" pieces of wood *
Sandpaper
Fine-tipped permanent marking pen, (e.g., Sharpie)
Acrylic or craft paint
Paintbrushes
Shellac or clear acrylic spray

* Make animals 3" long; people, 6" long; the manger, 4" long (note that you will turn the manger sideways). To make 4 people, 2 sheep, and a manger, you will need a board 34" long.

Whatcha Do

1. Sand the ends of the wood blocks.
2. Draw an outline of Joseph, Mary, and two shepherds, each on a 6" block.
3. Draw an outline of a sheep on each 3" block.
4. Turn the 4" block on its side and draw a manger on it.
5. Paint each figure.
6. Outline each figure with a fine paintbrush or black permanent fine-line marking pen.
7. Shellac or spray with a clear acrylic. **(An adult should do this outside, away from the children.)**

The figures should be kept very simple.

Children may wish to design each figure on paper first.

© 1992 Concordia Publishing House

Gospel in a Nutshell

Whatcha Need
A whole walnut
Paint (optional)
Glue
Ribbon
Fine-tipped permanent marking pen
Quilling paper

Whatcha Do
1. Paint the nut (optional).
2. Place glue along the "seam" of the walnut.
3. Press ribbon along the glue. Join ribbon ends at the top and make a loop for a hanger.
4. Use a permanent marking pen to write **John 3:16** on one side of the nut and your name on the other.
5. Write the words "For God so loved . . ." on a strip of quilling paper and glue it at the top where the ribbon meets. Place the end of the paper at the joint so it looks as if it's coming out of the walnut.

Variation: To make a Christmas ornament, paint the nut white, green, or red, and add a ribbon of the same color. Hang the decorated walnuts on dresser knobs, bedposts, or on peg shelves.
Make several of these and give them away to share the Gospel.

© 1992 Concordia Publishing House

Creation Shadow Cans

Whatcha Need

A tin can (small tuna fish or cat food size)
Craft paint (various colors)
Paintbrush
Blue or green spray paint (optional)
Items from nature
Glue
Cotton
A self-adhesive picture hanger (optional)

Whatcha Do

1. Clean and dry the can inside and out. (**An adult needs to make sure the can has no rough or sharp edges.**)
2. Paint the can a desired color (blue for water, green for forest). Spray paint is fast, but **must be used by an adult in a well-ventilated area.**
3. When the paint has dried, arrange items from nature inside the can. Glue the items in place.
4. Add cotton balls for clouds. Inside the can paint rainbows, stars, a sun, or whatever you would like to add to the scene.
5. Attach a picture hanger at the top of the can.
   This project can remind the children of our creator. It also allows for a lot of creativity. It is a good size for display on a student's shelf or windowsill.

© 1992 Concordia Publishing House

Wooden Wind Chimes

Use a variety of nails

IXOYE

Whatcha Need

A piece of wood, 1/4" thick (cut
  into the shape of a butterfly or
  fish) *
Sandpaper
Crayons
A plastic knife or hand pencil
  sharpener (optional)
Newsprint (not old newspaper!)
An iron
Plastic thread, fish line,
  or dental floss
Five large nails
Ribbon

*The fish was a secret symbol used by early Christians to tell others they believed in Jesus.

Whatcha Do

1. Before class, ask someone in your congregation who owns a jigsaw to cut out the wooden shapes and drill one hole at the top and five at the bottom of each shape.
2. Smooth the edges of the shape with sandpaper.
3. Color the shape with crayon (pressing very hard) or cover the shape with crayon shavings.
4. Place a couple of thicknesses of newsprint over the shape and iron with a hot iron. **(An adult should use the iron.)**
5. Use the fish line or dental floss to attach large nails to the bottom of the shape through the holes.
6. Use the ribbon to make a hanger, threading it through the hole at the top of the shape.

© 1992 Concordia Publishing House

And the Seed Grew

Whatcha Need

A natural sponge
Water
A variety of fast-sprouting seeds (lima beans, peas, etc.)
2 ribbons

Whatcha Do

1. Wet the sponge; squeeze out excess water. (Water should not be dripping from the sponge.)
2. Fill the holes in the sponge with seeds.
3. Tie one ribbon around the sponge, placing a bow on top. Knot the bow.
4. Attach the second ribbon to form a loop.
5. Hang the sponge in a window and watch the seeds grow.
6. Keep the sponge moist.

Use this project anytime you teach about the power of God's Word or when you study the parable of the sower. Remind older students that God often tells us that His Word is like seed—powerful and life-giving, even though we cannot always see its power.

© 1992 Concordia Publishing House

Handy Holder

Craft sticks

Ribbon

Glue

Styrofoam

Make as a gift for family & friends.

Whatcha Need

22 craft sticks
Glue
A variety of dry beans
Styrofoam rectangle (2-1/2" x 4")
Ribbon

beans

Give Thanks

My Devotion

Whatcha Do

1. Lay two craft sticks on a desk or tabletop parallel to one another and 2" apart.
2. Glue nine craft sticks to the parallel sticks horizontally to make a tight ladder as shown. All sticks must be touching.
3. Continue this process a second time, thus creating the two sides of the holder.
4. Use various dry beans to form appropriate words and designs.
5. Glue decorative ribbon around the Styrofoam base.
6. Push the ends of the holder into the base as shown.

This craft can hold a family devotional magazine and a pocket-size New Testament.

46

© 1992 Concordia Publishing House

"I Ate Jonah" and Other Fun Story Puzzles

Jonah
big fish - a man - a heart

Whatcha Need

Plywood, 8" x 12" (one piece per child)
Pencils
Sandpaper
Paint (three different colors, tempera or acrylic; if you use tempera, add a small amount of white glue to the paint)

Use the puzzles to tell and retell the Bible Stories.

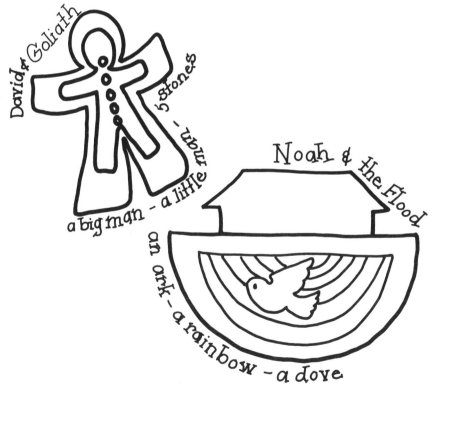

David & Goliath
5 stones
a big man - a little man

Noah & the Flood
an ark - a rainbow - a dove

Whatcha Do

1. Give the children an 8" x 12" piece of plywood and a pencil. Ask them to design a jigsaw puzzle based on the Bible story you are studying. Tell them that thin pieces may break while cutting, so they should try to draw simple pictures with thick pieces. No puzzle should have more than four pieces. As they design their puzzles, tell them that each piece should be contained in the next larger piece, so bigger pieces of the puzzle "eat up" the little pieces while you retell the story.
2. **After the children have drawn their design on the board, have an adult use a jigsaw to cut out the pieces.**
3. Sand and paint the puzzle pieces.

   Younger children can paint the puzzle pieces and retell the story. Older children can design their own pieces and then paint them once the puzzle is cut out.

© 1992 Concordia Publishing House

Wooden Angels

Wood Triangle

Wood ball

glue gun

Glue

Spanish moss

lace — rickrack

Wallpaper scraps

Twisted paper ribbon

Whatcha Need

A wooden equilateral triangle, 4" per side and 1/2"–3/4" thick
A wooden ball, about 1-1/2" in diameter
Marking pens or paint and brushes
Hot glue gun, wood glue, or white glue
Wallpaper scraps, scraps of fabric, rickrack and lace
Spanish moss (from a florist's shop)
A piece of twisted paper ribbon 9" long

Whatcha Do

Before class cut 1/2" off the top of the triangle. (Note: Perhaps you can find someone in your congregation who enjoys woodworking to help you prepare the triangles.)

1. Use marking pens or paint to put a face on the wooden ball.
2. Use wood glue or a hot glue gun to glue the wooden ball (head) to the triangle (body). **(Exercise close supervision if students will work with the glue gun. Otherwise, let an adult do this step in an area away from the children.)**
3. Use wallpaper, fabric, rickrack, or lace to decorate the angel's body.
4. Glue spanish moss to the head for hair.
5. Untwist the paper ribbon. Glue the ends together. Pinch it together in the center to form a bow (wings). Glue these to the back of the angel.

Use this project in connection with lessons dealing with angels as God's messengers or angels as they watch over us to protect us.

48

© 1992 Concordia Publishing House

Rubber Stamp Set

wood. foil . . . . . If you do not have an old inner tube – glue yarn on a wood block, making your favorite design.

Whatcha Need

Inner tube from a truck tire
Scissors
Empty spools or scraps of
two-by-fours, each 3"–4" long.
Rubber cement
Ink pads or paint

Print on paper. boxes . bags . cards . bookcovers

Paint

Ink Pad

Cards

Inner Tube

boxes

bags

Rubber Cement

yarn

Whatcha Do

1. Cut shapes, letters, numbers, or words from the piece of inner tube.
2. Glue these to the boards or spools with rubber cement. (Remember that letters, words, and numbers must be glued on backward to print correctly. Look at your design in a mirror before you cut it out!)
3. Use paint or ink to print.

© 1992 Concordia Publishing House

Sweet-Smelling Dough

Whatcha Need

- Applesauce
- Ground cinnamon, cloves, and nutmeg
- Cutting board
- Rolling pin
- Cookie cutters
- Spatula
- Tempera paint or fabric puff paints
- Yarn or ribbon

Whatcha Do

1. Mix 1/3 cup warm applesauce, 6 tablespoons cinnamon, 2 tablespoons cloves, and 2 tablespoons nutmeg together to form a ball.
2. Sprinkle some cinnamon onto a cutting board and roll the dough to about 1/4" thickness with a rolling pin.
3. Cut out the dough with cookie cutters, and make a hole in the top of each figure to use later for hanging.
4. Lift cutouts with a spatula and place them in a cool area to dry. Turn them often. The drying time is usually about 24 hours.
5. Decorate, adding words and names with tempera or fabric paint.
6. Add a hanger made from yarn or a ribbon.

© 1992 Concordia Publishing House

Tin Lid Ornaments

Whatcha Need

Lids from 12 oz. juice cans (the type that open by pulling off a plastic strip—these lids don't have rough edges)

Paper patterns made by teacher or students (see directions below)

Several thicknesses of newspaper

hammer

A thin nail

Thin ribbon

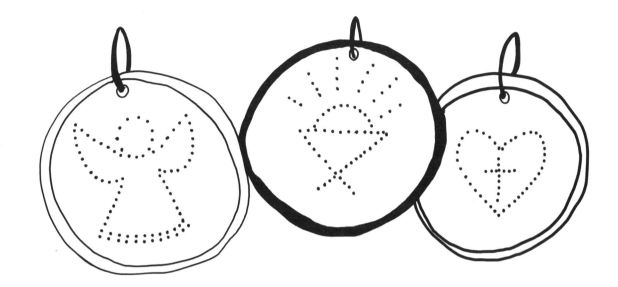

make patterns on paper

Whatcha Do

1. To make patterns, cut circles of paper that will fit inside the lids you are using. Draw designs with dots.
2. Place a pattern on a lid and place the lid on a pad of newspapers.
3. Use the hammer and nail to drive holes into the lid following your pattern. Note: After the children have put the holes in the lids, an adult should turn the lids over and flatten any rough edges with a hammer.
4. String a length of ribbon through a top hole. Tie the ribbon in a loop and hang the lid in a window so the light can shine through the design. Or hang the lid as an ornament on a Christmas tree.

© 1992 Concordia Publishing House

Glue Hangings

Whatcha Need

White glue

Powdered tempera paint or food coloring

Pattern of an object or symbol that relates to the day's lesson.

Waxed paper

Tissue paper or colored cellophane paper *(optional)*

Yarn

the glue back together.

If the glue separates, use a toothpick to spread the glue back together.

on the tissue before backing the glue shape.

"God so loved the world that He gave His one and only Son."

The surface must be flat.

Try abstract shapes. Write your favorite Bible verse

Whatcha Do

1. Color the glue with tempera paint or food coloring.*
2. Return the glue to the squeeze-bottle.
3. Give each child a pattern.
4. Place the pattern under the waxed paper, making certain your work surface is flat and even.
5. Squeeze the glue onto the waxed paper, following the lines of the pattern. (These lines will be thick and not exactly like the pattern.)
6. After the symbol is complete, squeeze additional glue across the design to strengthen the hanging.
7. Allow the design to dry 24–48 hours, depending on the humidity in your area.
8. Gently remove the design from the waxed paper.
9. Trace around the design on tissue paper or colored cellophane paper.
10. Cut the shape and glue tissue paper to the design.
11. Attach yarn and hang your creation in a window.

   * Precolored glue may also be purchased.

© 1992 Concordia Publishing House

Tissue-Paper Ornaments and Suncatchers

Whatcha Need

A variety of brightly-colored tissue paper

Colored marking pens

Patterns of objects or symbols relating to the
day's lesson (optional)

Scissors

Clear, shiny contact paper

Yarn or ribbon

Jesus ♡ me

Use as Christmas ornaments or suncatchers for Easter or Baptisms

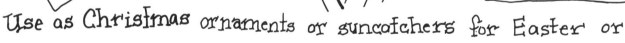

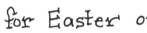

Whatcha Do

1. Cut tissue paper into pieces approximately 5" x 5".
2. Use marking pens to draw designs on the tissue paper. You may put patterns under the paper and trace them.
3. Cut out the design.
4. Cover both sides with contact paper. (Or laminate the designs, if you have access to a laminating machine.)
5. Trim off the excess contact paper, leaving a border of about 1/8".
6. Attach a yarn or ribbon hanger.

© 1992 Concordia Publishing House

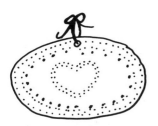

Pierced-Paper Promise Tree

Whatcha Need

Drawing paper or watercolor paper (white)

Pencil

Cookie cutters or cardboard patterns

Scissors

Old towels

A large needle

Marking pens, colored pencils

Plastic spice jar or other small, unbreakable container

Wet sand to fill container

Small branch that resembles a tree

Ribbon or yarn

Materials for decorating jar and cutouts (e.g., ribbon, stickers)

Whatcha Do

1. Use cookie cutters or cardboard patterns to trace shapes on paper. Cut them out.
2. Place these cutouts on a folded towel and use the needle to pierce holes along the edges. Follow a pattern or place the holes randomly.
3. Use marking pens or colored pencils to add a Bible verse, words that tell one of God's promises, or other appropriate words to the center of each cutout.
4. Place wet sand in the container and add the branch.
5. Tie the cutouts to the tree using ribbon or yarn.
6. Decorate the tree and container using items like stickers, ribbons, and glitter.

© 1992 Concordia Publishing House

Christian Calendar

Whatcha Need

A Bible

12 pieces of white paper, each 8" x 11"

Marking pens or crayons

13 pieces of construction paper, each 9" x 12"

Glue

12 calendar pages, each 8" x 11"

Hole punch

Hole reinforcements

2 ring clips

Whatcha Do

1. Select 12 Bible verses, one for each month.
2. Write one of the verses you have chosen on each of the white pieces of paper. Draw a picture to illustrate the verse on each page.
3. Glue each of these sheets to the center of a sheet of construction paper, thus framing each verse and illustration.
4. Glue a calendar page for a specific month upside down on the back side of each picture. (Note: The students can make these on pages you provide–each page divided into 35 squares. Or you may wish to duplicate calendar pages for them.)
5. Punch holes at the top and bottom of each piece of construction paper. Reinforce the holes. (Holes should be in the same place on all sheets of paper.)
6. Put the calendar pages in order and clip them together on the rings.

© 1992 Concordia Publishing House

Whatcha Need

An 8" paper plate, white
Marking pens or crayons
Scissors
Animal crackers
Glue

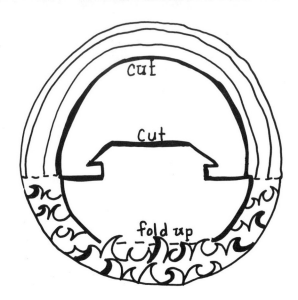

Noah's Ark

Whatcha Do

1. Draw a pattern on the paper plate as shown in diagram 1.
2. Color the rainbow, water, and ark.
3. Cut along the lines as shown.
4. Glue animal crackers to the ark.
5. Fold the ark and the rainbow up at the base of each to create a 3-D effect.

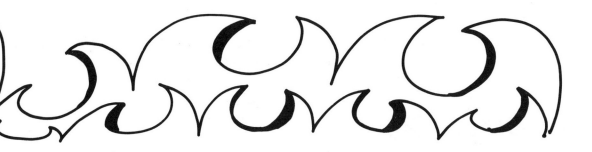

© 1992 Concordia Publishing House

Delightful Doorknobbers

© 1992 Concordia Publishing House

Whatcha Need

Construction paper in a variety of colors,
  2 sheets per doorknobber
  (one 4-1/2" x 12"; one 4" x 11")
Pencil
Scissors
Glue
Marking pens
Glitter, rickrack, sequins, buttons, jingle
  bells (*optional*)

Whatcha Do

1. Fold the smallest sheet of construction paper in half.
2. Draw one or two symmetrical shapes along the fold (hearts, crosses, crowns, flames, flowers, Christmas trees, butterflies, etc.). Be sure to leave room at the top for the doorknob hole.
3. Cut out the shapes.
4. Unfold the paper and glue it to a larger piece of a contrasting color.
5. Cut a hole near the top for the doorknob.
6. Decorate with marking pens and other materials.
7. Add a message or Bible verse from the lesson.

Note: These make cheery "get well" cards—something a little different in a hospital room. It's also a great way to share a message with neighbors, or just as a reminder of God's great love for us.

Swirling Paint and Paper

Use more than one color.

Use paper or light weight cardboard for cards, bookcovers or frames.

Dip bottles or jars into the paint.

Whatcha Need

Foil pan, 9" x 13"
Water
Oil-based enamel
  paints (craft stores
  sell small bottles)
Toothpicks
Watercolor paper
Tongs or tweezers

Use the painted paper as a background.

Whatcha Do

1. Fill the foil pan with 2–3" of water.
2. Use the toothpick to add small drops of paint to the water and swirl it. (Use one or two colors of paint.)
3. Gently lay a sheet of paper on top of the water, then lift the paper from the water with a tweezers or tongs.
4. Carefully shake off the excess water and set the paper aside to dry.
5. When the paper has dried, use it for cutouts, frames, or greeting cards. Decorate it with Bible verses, Christian symbols, or other witnessing messages.

© 1992 Concordia Publishing House

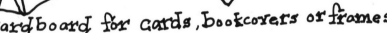

Paper-Bag Fish

Whatcha Need

White lunch-size paper bags
Watercolor paints
Paintbrushes
Marking pens
Construction paper
Glue
Newspaper
Rubber band
Hole punch
Yarn

The fish was a secert symbol used by early christians to tell others they believed in Jesus.

"make a school"

Make many more fish

IXθYE

Whatcha Do

1. Use paint, marking pens, and/or construction paper to decorate both sides of the bag.
2. Fold the bottom corners in, as shown, to make the head of the fish.
3. Use crumpled newspaper to stuff the bag about half full.
4. Use the rubber band to secure the top third of the bag to create the tail.
5. Punch a hole in the top and attach a loop of yarn to make a hanger.

© 1992 Concordia Publishing House

Pocket Hearts

Whatcha Need

Felt, sew-in interfacing, or construction paper (6" x 12" or 12" x 18")
Scissors
Glue or stapler
Lace, pom-poms, rickrack, buttons
Marking pens

fold

cut

2. fold

3. fold up   fold up

fold down

4.

We love because He first loved us.   God is ♥

fill your heart with flowers, cookies, and candies.

by grace...

Jesus loves you!

Whatcha Do

1. Fold the fabric (or paper) in half vertically.

2. Cut the top as shown in illustration 1. Unfold.

3. Fold the bottom up to the top and crease (see illustration 2).

4. Fold the lower right and left corners toward the center (see illustration 3).

5. Fold the top flap down and glue or staple it in place (see illustration 4).

6. Use lace, rickrack, pom-poms and/or buttons to decorate the heart.

7. Write messages about God's love and forgiveness or a Bible verse on the flap. Then give the heart away.

   Option: Fill the heart in with flowers, cookies, or candies.

© 1992 Concordia Publishing House

Whatcha Need

Paper for patterns
Pencil
Colorful pages from magazines or used church service folders
Scissors
String or yarn
Glue

Cut four identical pieces - tie together to make an 8 pointed star.

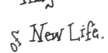

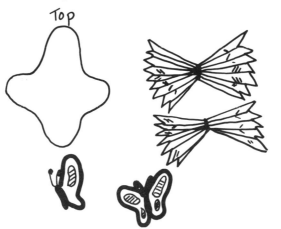

Top

Fold

magazine page

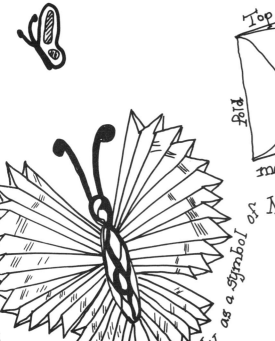

Christians use the butterfly as a symbol of New Life.

Whatcha Do

1. Draw two butterfly-wing patterns similar to those in the diagram .
2. Fold the magazine page or church folder in half vertically, keeping the colored side to the outside.
3. Trace the butterfly pattern onto the page and cut it out. Set the pattern aside.
4. Fanfold the wing you just made from top to bottom.
5. Repeat the procedure with the second pattern.
6. Cut out a body for the butterfly.
7. Place both fanfolded wings together and tie them in the center.
8. Glue the body in place.

Variation: Cut four identical pieces; tie them together and make an eight-pointed star.

© 1992 Concordia Publishing House

Contact-Paper Collage

Less expensive printed materials work best.

Whatcha Need

Clear contact paper (10" x 12")

Scissors

Paper or matte board frame (10" x 12")

Magazines and newspapers (a large selection)

Plastic tub or sink filled with hot, soapy water

Permanent marking pen

Whatcha Do

1. Cut contact paper to fit your frame.
2. Cut various shapes and sizes of pictures from the magazines or newspapers. Choose a collage theme (e.g., creation, God's people, showing Christian love).
3. Carefully pull the paper backing off the contact paper and place the *sticky side up* on a smooth, flat surface.
4. Carefully place the cutouts *facedown* on the sticky surface. Empty spaces are okay, but not necessary.
5. Now rub the back of each cutout very hard with the back of a spoon, a penny, or fingernail, being careful not to tear through the paper. **This is a very important step if the paper is to come off when soaked.**
6. When each cutout has been rubbed, place the collage in the hot, soapy water and let it soak for 15 minutes or more until the paper floats off, leaving a translucent picture. (Some pictures may be stubborn and require a gentle rubbing.)
7. Dry and frame your picture. Add Bible words or another Christian caption with a permanent marking pen.
8. The back will be sticky. You may wish to place an additional piece of contact paper on the back of the collage.

   Option: Older children can create a slide show using slide frames and smaller cutouts. Follow the same procedure as above.

© 1992 Concordia Publishing House

Whatcha Need

Drawing paper
Plastic tub or sink filled with water
Newspapers
Watercolor paints
Paintbrushes
A dark, fine-line marking pen

Whatcha Do

1. Place a piece of paper in water, then pull it out. Let the water drip off for a few seconds.
2. Lay the paper on a pad of old newspapers.
3. Using a paintbrush, drop and lightly brush paints of different colors onto the wet paper. The colors will blend together.
4. When the paint is thoroughly dry, use a dark marking pen to draw the Bible story on the background sheet you just made.
5. Frame the painting. (See "Fun with Frames," p. 23.)

Watercolor
and
Ink Bible Story

© 1992 Concordia Publishing House

"Bubbles, Bubbles, Bubbles" Place Cards

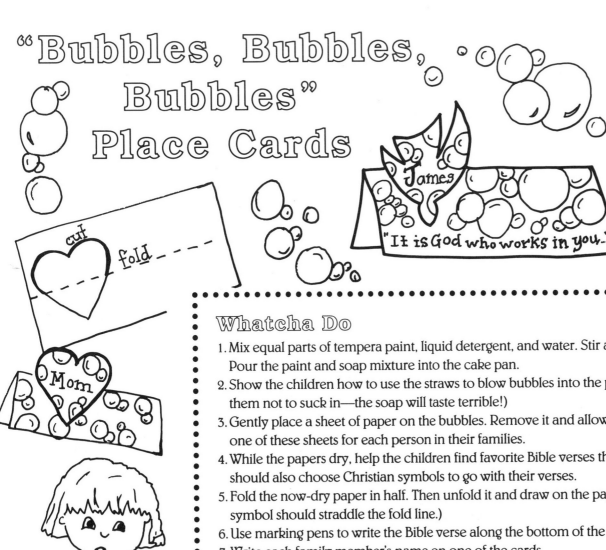

Whatcha Need

Paint and soap mixture (See step 1 below)
Cake pan
Straws
White construction paper or watercolor paper, approximately 4" x 4"
Bible
Marking pens
Scissors

Whatcha Do

1. Mix equal parts of tempera paint, liquid detergent, and water. Stir and allow it to sit for 2–3 hours before you use it. Pour the paint and soap mixture into the cake pan.
2. Show the children how to use the straws to blow bubbles into the pan. (Remind them to blow gently. Also remind them not to suck in—the soap will taste terrible!)
3. Gently place a sheet of paper on the bubbles. Remove it and allow it to dry. Tell the children they will need to make one of these sheets for each person in their families.
4. While the papers dry, help the children find favorite Bible verses they would like to share with their family. They should also choose Christian symbols to go with their verses.
5. Fold the now-dry paper in half. Then unfold it and draw on the paper the Christian symbol they have chosen. (The symbol should straddle the fold line.)
6. Use marking pens to write the Bible verse along the bottom of the place card.
7. Write each family member's name on one of the cards.
8. Cut into the back of the place card up to the symbol. Cut around the upper half of the symbol.
9. Refold the place card as before so that the upper half of the symbol is left standing to give a three-dimensional effect.

Variation: Use this process to make book covers or greeting cards, too, if you like.

64

© 1992 Concordia Publishing House

Bubble-print Place Mats

Whatcha Need

Old newspapers
Four small jars of bubble-blowing liquid with wands (from a toy store or discount department store)
Food coloring (four different colors)
Large pieces of white construction paper or drawing paper
Marking pens (*optional*)
Contact paper or access to a laminating machine (*optional*)

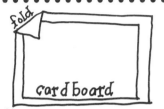

fold
card board
fold corners over - glue
fold edges over - glue.

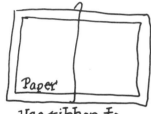

Paper
Use ribbon to secure the paper.

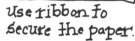

Prayer Journal
fold in half

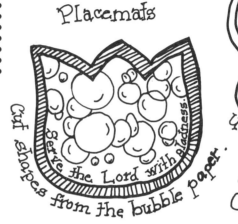

Placemats
Cut shapes from the bubble paper.
Serve the Lord with gladness.

He is Risen
Use makers to add scripture.
Cover with contact paper or laminate.
Cut out.

Whatcha Do

1. Cover the work area with newspapers.
2. Add approximately 1/2 bottle of food coloring to each jar of bubbles. Stir. (If you desire brighter, darker colors, add more food coloring.)
3. Lay the white paper on the newspaper. Gently blow bubbles onto the paper. As the bubbles pop, they will make a beautiful design on the paper.
4. Use the paper as a background sheet on which to illustrate Bible stories, design an artistic version of a Bible memory verse, or write a personal letter or Gospel message.

Note: *This is a great project to do outside if there is no wind. Several children can work in the same area allowing bubbles to drift onto one another's paper.*

The paper is great for greeting cards, book covers, or table place mats. You may want to cover book covers and place mats with clear contact paper or laminate them so they last longer.

© 1992 Concordia Publishing House

"God Loves His Children" Pull-Apart Pictures

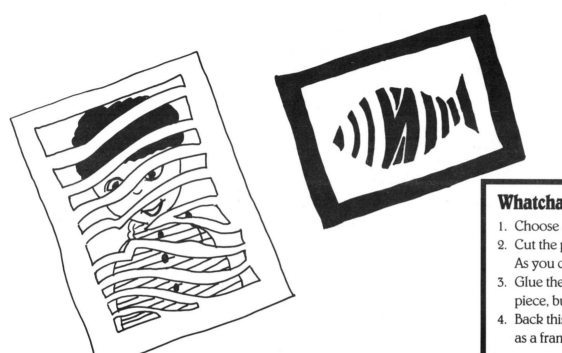

Whatcha Do

1. Choose a picture.
2. Cut the picture into narrow, curving strips or other interesting shapes. As you cut the picture apart, keep the pieces in order.
3. Glue the pieces onto a background paper leaving spaces between each piece, but assembling them so that the whole picture is recognizable.
4. Back this sheet with a larger piece of construction paper to serve as a frame.

Variation: This project can be adapted to include pictures of God's creation or of God's blessings. Younger children could use simple shapes rather than photos.

Whatcha Need

Pictures of people from magazines, newspapers, old bulletin covers, or lesson leaflet pictures
Scissors
Construction paper
Glue

© 1992 Concordia Publishing House

Bookmark

Whatcha Need

Watercolor paper, 2" x 7" strip
Marking pens
Clear contact paper or access to a laminating machine
Scissors
Hole punch
A narrow ribbon

draw a symbol on the bookmark

fold

cut

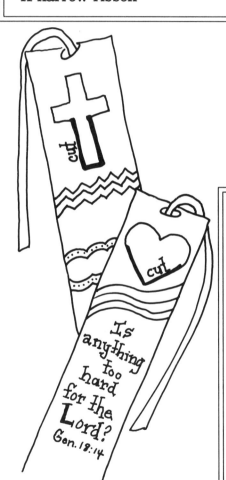

cut

cut

Is anything too hard for the Lord? Gen. 18:14

I will instruct you and teach you in the way you should go. Ps. 32:8

Whatcha Do

1. About 1" from the top of the paper, draw a simple Christian symbol (anchor, cross, butterfly) and color it with a marking pen.
2. Decorate the rest of the bookmark. Write an appropriate Bible passage on the bookmark.
3. Cover both sides of the bookmark with clear contact paper or laminate it.
4. Fold the bookmark in half lengthwise (but do not crease it) so you can cut along the outline of the bottom half of the symbol you colored in. (See the illustration.)
5. Punch a hole in the top of the bookmark.
6. Tie a ribbon (or two ribbons) through the hole.

© 1992 Concordia Publishing House

"God's Gifts to Me" Crest

fold

cut

cover the crest with foil

cut out a cross for the center of the crest.

Whatcha Do

1. Help the children recognize the gifts God gives them. Discuss ways they can use these gifts to serve other people.
2. Cut a crest shape from poster board.
3. Cut aluminum foil to fit the crest. Glue it onto the crest.
4. Cut and glue a crest-shaped piece of construction paper to the back of the crest.
5. Cut and glue a large cross on the crest.
6. Glue your picture to the center of the crest.
7. Print theme such as, "God's Gifts to Me" on paper and glue it above or below the photograph.
8. Have each child color, cut, and glue pictures of their interests, abilities, and talents to the open sections on the crest.
9. Make holes in the top of the crest and tie a ribbon through it for hanging.

Whatcha Need

Poster board
Scissors
Aluminum foil
Glue
Construction paper
Photograph of each child
Colored marking pens or crayons
Ribbon

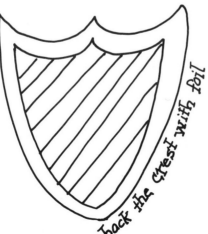

back the crest with foil

68

© 1992 Concordia Publishing House

Plaster Paperweights

Plaster of Paris

water

Pour mixture into a bag – leave the bag open – squeeze and hold.

Let your light shine.

Jesus is the Rock

Whatcha Need

Plaster of paris

Water and bowl

Sturdy plastic bags

Sandpaper

Paint or marking pens

Shellac or spray acrylic *(optional)*

Felt

Scissors

Glue

Whatcha Do

1. Mix plaster according to directions for a quick set.
2. Pour it into bags and squeeze it to create an interesting shape. (Do not twist-tie the bag; simply hold it closed.)
3. Hold the plaster in place until it begins to harden.
4. When it has set, remove it from the bag.
5. Use sandpaper to smooth any rough edges.
6. Use paints or marking pens to decorate it.
7. Spray your sculpture with acrylic spray or shellac. (An adult should do this in a well-ventilated area away from the students.)
8. Cut a piece of felt to fit the bottom of the sculpture. Glue it in place.

© 1992 Concordia Publishing House

Rock Paperweight

plaster of paris

rock

press the rock into the sand

shell

gravel or sand

pour the plaster over the rock

when set, pull the carton off.
Dust the sand off.

Whatcha Need

The bottom half of a pint milk carton

Sand

An interesting rock about 1-1/2" to 2"
    across, one large shell, or several small shells

Plaster of paris

Permanent marking pens or craft paint

Felt

Scissors

Glue

Whatcha Do

1. Cover the bottom of the milk carton with approximately 3/4" of sand.
2. Press the rock or the shell(s) into the sand. The side you want to show in the finished product should be buried in the sand.
3. Mix the plaster of paris according to directions for a quick set.
4. Pour an inch or so of plaster over the rock or shell(s) and sand. Allow the plaster to harden and dry.
5. Remove the plaster and the rock or shell(s) now embedded in it from the milk carton and brush off the sand.
6. Use craft paints or marking pens to write a Bible verse or another Christian message around the base of the paperweight.
7. Cut a piece of felt to fit the base of the paperweight and glue it in place.

Jesus the rock!

© 1992 Concordia Publishing House

Plant Pals

Whatcha Need

Tagboard or heavy paper
Brightly colored marking pens
Scissors
Glue stick
Clear contact paper or access to a laminating machine
Glue gun and glue
Dowels (approximately 1/16" in diameter and
    each cut to 12" in length)
Ribbon

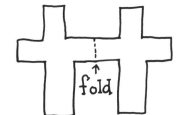

fold

fold

Jesus forgives me.

Whatcha Do

1. Draw doubled outlines of symbols on the tagboard. (A cross, heart, or simple tulip are outlines that work well.)
2. Have the children color each outline with bright colors. Print an appropriate Bible verse on one side.
3. Fold and trim the outlines. Use a dab of glue stick inside the top of the cutout to help hold the sides together until you laminate.
4. Laminate the cutouts or cover both sides with clear contact paper.
5. Trim the plastic from around the completed shapes approximately 1/8" from the edges, except at the bottom. The bottom of the shape should be trimmed so that it is even with the tagboard.
6. Carefully separate the tagboard at the bottom and squirt a dab of hot glue inside. **(An adult should do this.)** Then insert a dowel and press the tagboard closed over the glue and the dowel.
7. Trim your plant pals with ribbon as shown.

© 1992 Concordia Publishing House

Dough Plant Pals

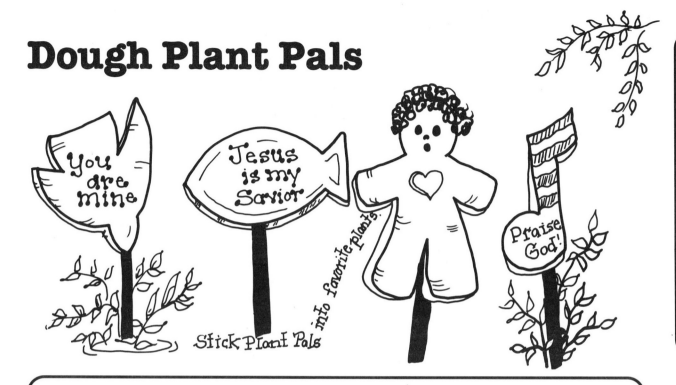

You are mine

Jesus is my Savior

Stick Plant Pals into favorite plants.

Praise God!

Whatcha Need

Dough in a variety of colors *
Rolling pin
Cookie cutters (heart, cross, butterfly, animals, flowers, etc.)
Foil-covered cookie sheet
Forks, toothpicks, and a garlic press
A wooden dowel, 1/16" in diameter and 12" long, or a shish-kabab skewer
Paint
Paintbrushes
Spray acrylic or shellac

Whatcha Do

1. Roll dough to 1/2" thick. Use a cookie cutter or form shapes by hand. Place them on a foil-covered cookie sheet.
2. Decorate the shapes using forks, toothpicks, and/or dough squeezed through a garlic press. Break off small bits of colored dough and use it as decorative matter, too.
3. Insert the dowel or skewer into the shape.
4. Bake at 250 degrees for 1–2 hours or until the shapes are hard.
5. Cool and paint the shapes as desired.
6. Spray the shapes with acrylic spray. (Three or four coats will give the shapes a very nice finish.) **As always, spray in a well-ventilated area, away from the children.**

*Dough:

Mix 2 c. flour, 1 c. salt, 1 c. warm water, and food coloring. (Add the food coloring to the water before you add the flour.) Knead the dough until very smooth, adding extra flour or water as needed. Store the dough in a plastic bag.

© 1992 Concordia Publishing House

Soda-Pop-Bottle Puppets

Whatcha Need

A plastic soda pop bottle (2 liter size)

Collage materials (e.g., yarn, buttons, paper scraps, fabric scraps, cotton balls, pom-poms)

Glue or hot glue gun

24"–36" dowel approximately 1/2" in diameter

Cellophane tape

-children-friends-teachers-

-a Samaritan-disciples-

Kings-shepherds—-Joseph-Mary-

Whatcha Do

1. Turn the bottle upside-down.
2. Use collage materials to decorate it. For hair, use 30 strands of yarn, 12"–18" long. Tie the shank of yarn in the center. Glue it to the bottom (now top) of the bottle. To make arms, use cones or rolls of paper. Glue these to the sides of the bottle.
3. Insert the dowel into the bottle as shown and tape it in place.

© 1992 Concordia Publishing House

Tube Puppets

Set up a table of collage materials and encourage the children to create their own Bible characters. Use the puppets to tell and retell the Bible stories.

Whatcha Need

Paper towel tubes
Miscellaneous items to decorate puppets
   (e.g., buttons, ribbons, cotton balls)
Construction paper, wallpaper,
   or fabric scraps
Glue
Brown or white strips of paper approximately 3" x 4"
Marking pens
Yarn

Use cotton balls to make sheep.

Try foil for the King's crown.

Whatcha Do

1. Use construction paper, wallpaper, fabric scraps, and other collage materials to decorate the paper towel tubes.
2. Use a strip of brown or white paper at the top of the tube to make the puppet's face. Add the facial features with a marking pen.
3. Glue yarn to the top for hair.

© 1992 Concordia Publishing House

Stick Puppets

Whatcha Need

Heavy paper or tagboard
Scissors
Marking pens
Collage materials (e.g., buttons, yarn, fabric scraps, beads, magazine pictures)
Paint-stirrer sticks or tongue depressors

Whatcha Do

1. Cut paper or tagboard to the approximate size you want the puppets to be.
2. Use marking pens and collage material to create puppets to tell today's Bible story or to make real-life applications of Biblical truths.
3. Cut out the puppets and glue them to paint-stirrer sticks or to tongue depressors.

Ask the children to make the characters from the Bible Stories. Use the puppets to tell the story.

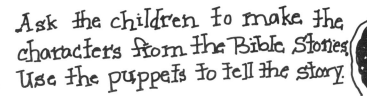

© 1992 Concordia Publishing House

Box Puppets

Whatcha Need

Small raisin boxes or gelatin boxes
Scissors
Construction paper or aluminum foil
Glue
Miscellaneous items to decorate puppets (e.g., buttons, yarn, puff paints, colored glue)
Craft sticks

Encourage the children to create their own characters.

Whatcha Do

1. Cut the top flaps off the boxes.
2. Cover the boxes with construction paper or foil. (Have younger children simply cover the front and back; leave the sides and bottom as they are.)
3. Use yarn, buttons, colored glue, paints, and whatever other glorious junk you can find to make faces on the boxes.
4. Glue the craft stick to the inside of the box or place the open part of the box on your fingers and use the box as a finger puppet.

Note: Gelatin boxes work well with the craft sticks. Raisin boxes are small enough for use with fingers.

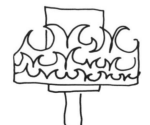
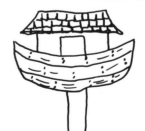

© 1992 Concordia Publishing House

© 1992 Concordia Publishing House

Whatcha Need

Heavy paper (e.g., construction paper)

Scissors

Collage materials (buttons, beads, glitter, sequins, yarn, cotton balls, etc.)

Marking pens

Glue

folded to make them stand.

Keep the puppets slightly

fold

shepherd

fold

King

fold

angel

fold

manger

fold

lamb

fold

fold

Simple Puppets

fold

fold

fold

Encourage children to use their

imagination in dressing the puppets.

Whatcha Do

1. Use the patterns on p. 109 to make the puppet figures. Fold your heavy paper in half, trace the pattern and cut out the figure.
2. Open the figure and decorate it to make a puppet character. The fold will allow the puppets to stand.
3. Encourage the children to create their own patterns for additional puppets.

   Young children love to act out stories using puppets, especially puppets they have made. Older children's puppets will become more detailed.

   You may use these puppets to tell or review Bible stories, or to act out life-related applications of Bible truths.

© 1992 Concordia Publishing House

Stand-up Puppets

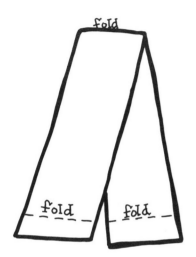   

Whatcha Need

Strips of heavy paper
  (e.g., construction paper)
Scissors
Collage materials (buttons,
  rickrack, pipe cleaners, yarn,
  fabric or wallpaper scraps)
Glue or glue sticks
Marking pens
Cellophane tape

Whatcha Do

1. To make one puppet, fold a strip of paper in half.
2. Fold the bottom edge of the paper over approximately 2". This will be the base of the puppet.
3. Draw the puppet shape desired. The head must touch the top and the feet must stop at the bottom fold.
4. Keeping the paper folded, cut out the outline of the puppet, making sure not to cut the top fold.
5. Use collage materials and marking pens to decorate the puppet, front and back.
6. Refold the bottom to form a base; tape it in place.
7. Repeat this procedure to make more puppets.

© 1992 Concordia Publishing House

Pentecost Sculpture

Whatcha Need

Two wire coat hangers

Plaster of paris

Bottom half of a half-gallon milk carton

Cardboard or wooden dove and flames

Paint or marking pens

Foil (optional)

String or yarn

Whatcha Do

1. Bend the hangers into interesting shapes. To do this, pull each hanger into a diamond shape then twist it slightly.
2. Mix plaster of paris according to directions and pour it into the milk carton. Secure the hangers in the plaster, holding them in place until set.
3. Decorate the dove and flames with paints or marking pens, or cover them with foil.
4. Remove the milk carton from plaster. Decorate the plaster base using marking pens or paint. Write a Bible passage around the base.
5. Hang the dove and flames from the hangers.

Variations: New life theme (butterflies); Christmas symbols; *God cares for my family* symbols

© 1992 Concordia Publishing House

Nail Sculpture

Whatcha Need

A piece of soft wood at least 1" thick
Pencil
Nails
Hammer
String, rubber bands, yarn, or thin colored wire

Whatcha Do

1. Ask the students to draw a Christian symbol or a simple design in keeping with the lesson on the wood.
2. Hammer nails into the wood along the design lines. Nails should be evenly spaced.
3. Weave rubber bands, yarn, string, or wire around the nails to create the design. Each design will be different, depending upon the pattern the weaver chooses.

© 1992 Concordia Publishing House

Stick Sculpture

Whatcha Need

Patterns for Christian symbols
Waxed paper
Sticks, sticks, and more sticks
Hot glue guns
Raffia or twine

Whatcha Do

1. Place a pattern for a Christian symbol underneath a sheet of waxed paper.
2. Break and arrange small sticks on the patterns.
3. Use a glue gun to glue the sticks together to make the shape you are working with. (Adults must supervise and help with the use of the hot glue gun.)
4. Reinforce the glued areas by knotting pieces of raffia at all joints as shown.
5. *Option:* Attach the figures you make to a larger tree branch to make a mobile.

The star reminds us of God's greatest gift to us—Jesus.
The cross reminds us of Jesus' death for our sins.
The triangle reminds us of the Trinity—Father, Son, and Holy Spirit—the three persons of the Godhead.

© 1992 Concordia Publishing House

"How Sweet the Name of Jesus Sounds"
Cube Cross

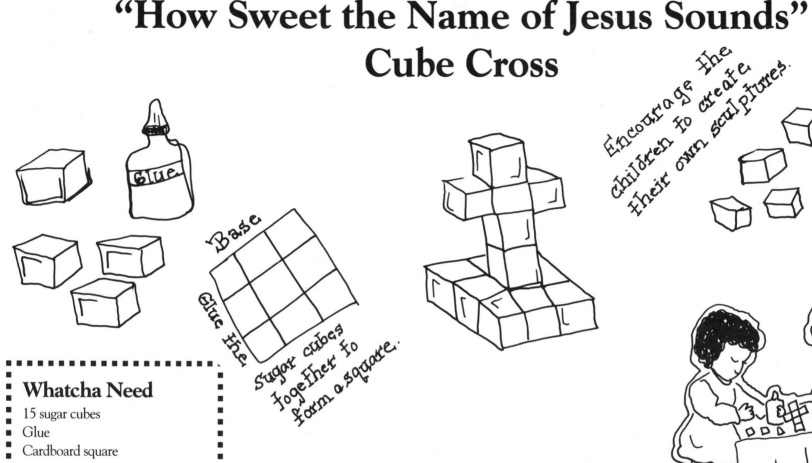

Encourage the children to create their own sculptures.

Base

Glue the sugar cubes together to form a square.

Whatcha Need

15 sugar cubes
Glue
Cardboard square

Whatcha Do

1. Glue three sugar cubes in a row. Make three rows to form a square.

2. Glue these together. Then glue this to a piece of cardboard to form the base.

3. Glue a cube atop the center cube of the base. Then glue three more cubes on it, building up.

4. When the glue dries, glue one additional cube on each side of the second cube from the top to form a cross.

© 1992 Concordia Publishing House

Make a Mold

Fill candy molds with papier-mache to make flowers.

My heart belongs to Jesus

Whatcha Need

Gelatin molds, cake molds, or plastic candy molds
Cooking oil spray
Newspaper (cut or torn into 1" strips)
Flour and water (mixed to the consistency of heavy cream)
Paint
Ribbons, yarn, buttons, etc.

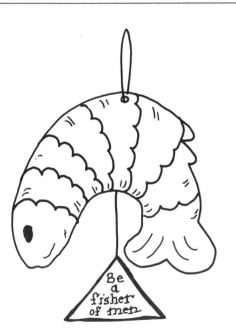

Be a fisher of men

Whatcha Do

1. Spray the mold with cooking oil. You can use either side of the mold, depending upon whether you want the finished product to be concave or convex.
2. Dip strips of newspaper in the flour/water mixture and place them carefully in the mold. Continue adding several layers of this papier-mâché to the mold in this same way.
3. If you are using small candy molds, make a ball of papier-mache and press it into the mold.
4. Allow figures to dry 24–48 hours, then gently pull them away from the mold.
5. Paint and decorate the piece of art.

Option: Use colored tissue paper in place of the newspaper when using small candy molds. The mixture will feel like slime, which will delight the children. The end product will not have to be painted.

© 1992 Concordia Publishing House

Witness Windsock

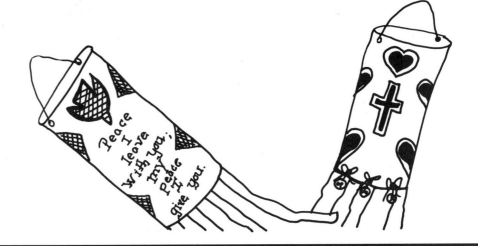

Whatcha Need

A piece of construction paper,
   12" x 18"

Scissors

Foil, cellophane, or contrasting
   colors of construction paper,
   12" x 18"

Glue or glue stick

Tape

Marking pens

Contact paper or access to a
   laminating machine

Florist, plastic, or foil ribbon

Stapler

Hole punch

Yarn

Jingle bells

Whatcha Do

1. Fold the piece of construction paper into fourths, vertically.
2. On the fold lines, draw symbols that tell people you are a Christian (hearts, fish, cross, butterfly, etc.). Be sure to discuss the meaning of each symbol with the class.
3. Carefully cut out the shapes. Then open the paper and glue pieces of foil, cellophane, or construction paper to the back of the open spaces you just made to create silhouettes of the symbols on the windsock.
4. Put a piece of tape all the way across the top and all the way across the bottom edges along the back side of the wind sock. This will reinforce the holes you will make in steps 9 and 10.
5. Use marking pens to decorate the front side of the windsock. Use an important biblical truth or a Bible verse that relates to the lesson.
6. Cover both sides of the windsock with contact paper or laminate it. This will allow the windsock to hang outside as a witness to all for a long time.
7. Staple, tape, or glue 8–11 ribbons along the bottom, inside edge.
8. Roll the windsock into a cylinder and staple or tape in place. (Supervise older students carefully. Do not let younger children use the stapler themselves.)
9. Punch two holes at the top edge of the windsock and attach yarn as a hanger.
10. Punch holes along the bottom edge of the windsock and tie on the jingle bells.

   Hang the windsock outside to tell all who come to visit that Jesus lives in your home.

© 1992 Concordia Publishing House

Whatcha Need

Fabric (muslin or felt)
Pinking shears
Pencil
Fabric paints
Thin ribbon
Glue
Pins
Needle and thread
Polyester fiberfill

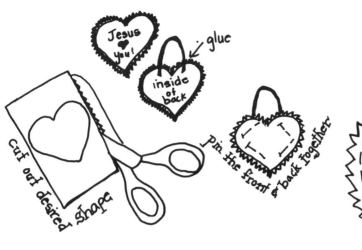

Painted-Fabric Hanging

Whatcha Do

1. Cut a shape (e.g., cross, heart, fish) from a double thickness of fabric using a pinking shears.
2. Lightly draw another shape on the fabric, using a pencil. Paint it with fabric paint.
3. Glue the ribbon to the inside of the back piece of fabric. Allow the glue to dry.
4. Pin the shapes together.
5. Sew the two shapes together by hand, leaving a small section open.
6. Stuff the shape with fiberfill to the desired fullness.
7. Sew the opening by hand.

Variations: This project can also be used as a hanging from a shelf or doorknob, or as a necklace.

Note: If you use the fish symbol, explain its meaning. The fish was a secret symbol used by Christians in the early church to identify one another. They used the Greek word for fish in an acrostic—these letters were the first letters in the Greek words for Jesus Christ, God's Son, Savior.

© 1992 Concordia Publishing House

Whatcha Need

12 mini-pretzels
Craft glue
Clear acrylic spray *(optional)*
2" length of ribbon

Prayer Prompters

Whatcha Do

1. Place four pretzels in a circle, their edges touching. Glue them in place.
2. Glue a second row of four pretzels on top of the circle, staggering them as shown.
3. Glue a third circle of pretzels atop the second, staggering them as before.
4. If you want to preserve this craft, spray it with clear acrylic. **(An adult should do this in a well-ventilated area away from the children.)**
5. When the glue or acrylic spray has dried, weave ribbon through the arms of the pretzels. Join the ends of the ribbon and tie them together.

Note: Christians in centuries gone by used to fold their arms over their chests in a pretzel-like shape when they prayed. Since then, the pretzel has become a reminder of prayer and a symbol for it.

This craft can remind students to pray, especially to intercede for others.

© 1992 Concordia Publishing House

Prayer Ribbon

Whatcha Need

Vinyl
Scissors
Permanent marking pens
Florist ribbon, 1" x 24"
Gold-colored ring
Glue

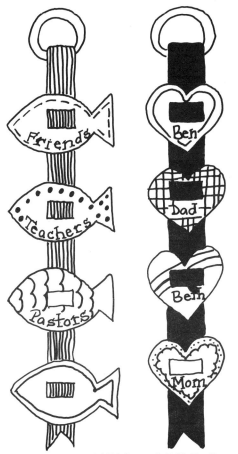

Whatcha Do

1. Cut four 4" hearts from the vinyl. If the children measure and cut carefully, a piece of vinyl 12" square should be more than enough.
2. Fold the hearts in half and carefully cut two slits across the center of each as shown.
3. On the first heart print a Bible verse about prayer (e.g., "Call upon Me" Ps. 50:15).
4. On the additional hearts, write the names of people for whom you can pray.
5. Use marking pens to decorate the hearts. Oil-based, permanent marking pens will write on vinyl. Remind the children to work with the marking pens carefully. The ink in them will stain their clothing!
6. Weave the ribbon through the hearts.
7. Glue the gold-colored ring to the top of the prayer ribbon and hang it on the wall as a reminder and invitation.

Variation: Use crosses or other shapes instead of hearts.

© 1992 Concordia Publishing House

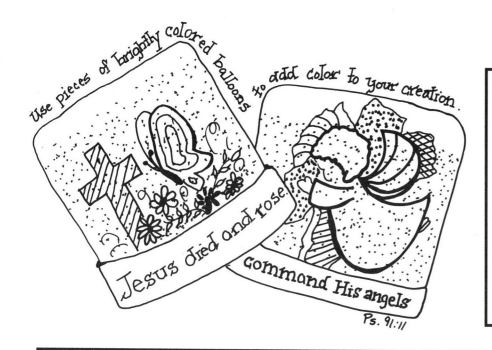

Use pieces of brightly colored balloons to add color to your creation

Jesus died and rose

command His angels

Ps. 91:11

Whatcha Need

Elmer's Silicone Rubber Sealer or other waterproof glue
Paper plates
Craft sticks
Variety of colored plastic lids from coffee, cans of powdered drink mix, etc.
Scissors
Waterproof permanent marking pens
Bouillon jar or baby food jar with lid
Glitter
Mineral oil or inexpensive baby oil
Electricians' tape
Tagboard or poster board

Whatcha Do

1. Place a puddle of silicone glue on a paper plate. You will need one plate for every two children. Give each child a craft stick to use in applying glue.
2. Cut shapes from plastic lids and glue them together to create a picture or design that will fit in the jar lid. Note that the figure should stand upright from the lid. Also note that the children can use a water proof marking pen to add extra color and design elements, but remember that permanent marking pens like these will stain clothing and tabletops, etc. Take precautions to prevent this.
3. Glue the plastic creation to the inside of the jar lid and allow it to dry.
4. Place about 1/4 teaspoon of glitter in the jar, then fill it almost full with mineral or baby oil.
5. Spread some silicone glue around the inside lip of the lid and screw the lid on the jar tightly.
6. For extra security, cover the seam with electricians' tape.
7. Glue a piece of tagboard around the lid to cover the tape. On it, write favorite Bible words.

Make-and-Shake Glitter Jar

© 1992 Concordia Publishing House

Note or Recipe Cardholder

Whatcha Need

- Clip clothespin
- Craft or acrylic paint
- Paintbrush (very small)
- Small tiles (from a tile store)
- Ribbon (very narrow)
- Glue
- Magnet strip

clothespin

ribbon

glue

magnet

tile

The peace of God, passes all understanding

"Be still, and know that I am God!" Ps. 46:10

set on a counter to hold a recipe – place on the refrigerator to hold messages.

Whatcha Do

1. Paint the clip clothespin.
2. Use the paint to decorate the tile.
3. Glue the ribbon around the outside edge of the tile.
4. Glue the clothespin to the back of the tile. The clip end needs to be at the top as shown in the illustration.
5. Glue a magnet strip to the back of the clothespin. Make sure the magnet strip is strong enough to hold the clothespin and tile securely to a metal surface.

When it's completed, use the project to hold messages on the refrigerator or set it up on a counter to hold recipes.

© 1992 Concordia Publishing House

Soap Painting

Whatcha Need

Paper
Pencil
A large, white bar of soap
Large nail *(optional)*
Paint
Paintbrush or cotton swabs
Fine-tipped marking pens

New Life in Christ.

God made the...

King of Kings

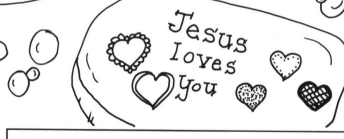

Jesus loves you

Whatcha Do

1. Sketch a simple Christian design on a piece of paper.
2. Draw the design on the soap with a pencil or nail. Press hard enough to make a slight depression in the soap. Use the tip of a paintbrush or cotton swab with a small amount of paint to fill in the design.
3. Add lettering with a fine-tipped marking pen.

   Use these soaps as thank-you gifts to parents or as witnessing gifts to shut-ins and the elderly.

© 1992 Concordia Publishing House

Weaving Mobile

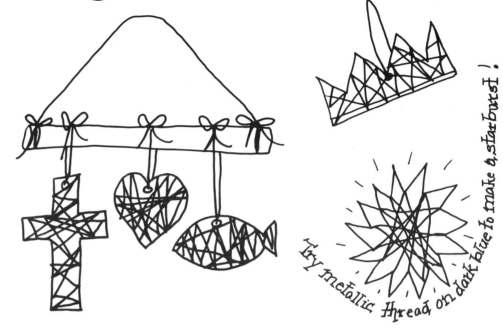

Try metallic thread on dark blue to make a starburst!

Whatcha Need

Sturdy cardboard or poster board
Scissors
Sparkly yarn or heavy metallic thread
Hole punch
A dowel, 12" long
Marking pens *(optional)*

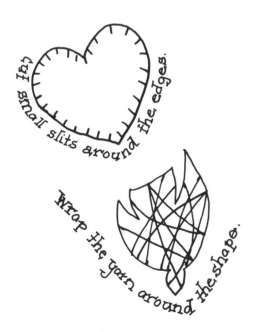

Cut small slits around the edges.

Wrap the yarn around the shape.

Whatcha Do

1. Cut shapes from the cardboard that fit in with the day's Bible story theme.
2. Cut small slits around each shape, each approximately 1/4"–1/2" apart.
3. Begin wrapping the shape with sparkling yarn or metallic thread. Use the slits to hold the yarn in place. Each shape will look a little different, depending on where you've placed the slits.
4. Punch a hole in the top of each figure and tie the shape to the dowel. Note that you will want the shapes each to hang at a different level.
5. Attach yarn to both ends of the dowel to make a hanger.
6. *Optional: Older students could use marking pens to add Bible verses or phrases that correlate with the lesson.*

© 1992 Concordia Publishing House

"Promise" Rainbow Weaving

Whatcha Need

Heavy cardboard frame
    or matte frame
Hole punch
Ruler
Yarn
Long, thin scraps of material,
    yarn, or raffia
    (rainbow colors)
Marking pens

Whatcha Do

1. Punch holes along the top and bottom of the frame. Use the ruler to line them up. There should be the same number of holes at the top and bottom.
2. Measure the distance from the top to the bottom, and then multiply by the number of holes. Add 15. This is the length, in inches, of the yarn you will use.
3. String the yarn through the holes. This should be tight, but not tight enough to bow the frame. Knot the string at the first and last hole.
4. Using the scraps of material, yarn, or raffia, weave an interesting design.
5. Use marking pens to title the weaving.

This project can help students recall God's promises to His people after the flood.

Hint: Many frame shops give away miscut matte boards.

© 1992 Concordia Publishing House

God's Creation Weaving

Knot in the back

Loop the twine behind the slits.

GOD CREATED

it was good

Use as many different items from nature as you can find.

Whatcha Need

A piece of cardboard or matte board, approximately 8" x 10" *

Scissors

Ruler

Twine

Tape

A strip of ribbon or construction paper 1/2" x the width of the weaving

Marking pens

Items from nature (e.g., long grasses, weeds, dried flowers, feathers, long pine needles, wheat, thin twigs)

Yarn or raffia of various colors *(optional)*

Whatcha Do

1. Cut an equal number of 1/4" slits along the top and bottom of the cardboard. Slits should be evenly spaced. (You may wish to use a ruler to line them up.)
2. Knot a long piece of twine at one end. Slip the twine into the first slit. (The knot will hold the twine in place.)
3. Pull the twine down to the bottom slit, slip it into place and return twine to the second slit at the top. Continue across the cardboard to make a loom.
4. Knot the twine at the back of the last slit or tape to the back of the cardboard. Keep the twine tight.
5. On the ribbon or construction paper, print "Then God said, 'Let the land produce vegetation,'" or "God created . . . it was good."
6. Weave the items from nature and the message across the loom.
7. Add a few extra strands of yarn or raffia to add color.
8. Tape a loop of twine to the back of the loom to make a hanger.

* Frame shops will often give teachers slightly marred or mismeasured matte boards at no charge.

© 1992 Concordia Publishing House

Witness Weaving

Pull strands of burlap from the fabric to form a cross.

Weave the gold and blue ribbon through the burlap.

Whatcha Need

Burlap, 6" x 12"
Ribbon, 5/8" wide; 22" gold and 44" of another color
A wooden dowel about 7" long, as small in diameter as possible
Ribbon for hanging

Whatcha Do

1. Remove a few threads from the center of the burlap. (Pull gently yet firmly.)
2. Weave a 15" piece of gold ribbon through this to make a "ladder," skipping under and over the burlap threads as desired. (E.g., you may wish to count by fives, going over five threads and then under five threads, and so on until you reach the end.)
3. Remove threads to make a cross bar area approximately one-third of the way down from the top of the banner.
4. Weave 7" of gold ribbon through this area in the same way you did for step 2.
5. Trim the ends of the ribbon. The basic cross is complete.
6. Use the colored ribbon to proceed in the same way down each side of the gold ribbon to enhance the cross.
7. Weave the dowel through the top part of the banner. Be sure to weave it behind the cross. Attach ribbon to the ends of the dowel to create a hanger.

This makes a great personal banner. It can get really intricate and sophisticated-looking, too!

© 1992 Concordia Publishing House

"Joseph's Coat of Many Colors"

cut various shapes from construction paper. Weave contrasting colors through the shapes.

Whatcha Need

Construction paper of different colors (9" x 12" or 12" x 18")
Scissors
Glue
Marking pens

Whatcha Do

1. Let each child choose a variety of pleasing colors of construction paper.
2. For the background, draw Joseph's coat on a piece of construction paper.
3. Cut approximately six vertical lines in the mid-section of the coat. (If you like, you can also cut four thinner lines into each sleeve.)
4. Cut several strips of paper, approximately 1" wide and in a color that contrasts with your "coat." (If you've decided to work with sleeves, use 1/2" strips for this.)
5. Weave the strips in and out, securing each end with glue. Trim off any excess.
6. When you have woven all the strips, use a marking pen to outline the coat. Add other details too.

Note: Young children will find larger paper easier to handle.

Variations: Adapt this project to any Bible story subject. Or use it as you work with simple Christian symbols.

Paper Weaving

95

© 1992 Concordia Publishing House

Witness License Plates

Whatcha Need

Fluorescent-colored tagboard, 3" x 8"
Watercolor marking pens
Foil paper *(optional)*
Glitter, sequins
Clear contact paper or access to a laminating machine
Hole punch
Pipe cleaner

Whatcha Do

1. Design a license plate on tagboard, using creative spelling or pictures to witness to others of Christ's love (e.g., "JLMTIK" *).
2. Use watercolor marking pens, foil paper, glitter, and similar items to decorate the license plate. Allow it to dry. (**Note:** Permanent marking pens will bleed into the contact paper after a time. Use watercolor marking pens for this project.)
3. Laminate the license plate, or cover it, front and back, with clear contact paper.
4. Punch two holes in the plate. Use the pipe cleaner to attach the plate to a bike.

*Jesus **L**oves **M**e **T**his **I** **K**now

© 1992 Concordia Publishing House

Pencil or Straw Toppers

Whatcha Need

Tagboard
Marking pens or paints
Scissors
A pencil or a soda straw
Clear contact paper or access to a
   laminating machine (optional)

King of Kings

Jesus Christ God's Son, Savior

Angels watching over me.

fold and cut slits

Fold

Fold

Whatcha Do

1. Use the patterns in the back pages of this guide to make hearts, crosses, butterflies, fish, or doves on a piece of tagboard. Cut these out.
2. Use marking pens or paints to decorate the shapes.
3. Fold and cut as shown in the illustration.
4. Place each topper on a pencil or straw.
5. Option: Laminate the toppers or cover them with clear contact paper, then recut slits.

These toppers can serve as inexpensive tools for sharing the Gospel with others.

© 1992 Concordia Publishing House

2.

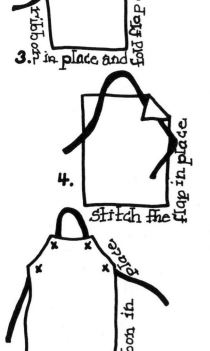

3. Lay the ribbon in place and fold flap over

4. Stitch the flap in place

5. stitch the ribbon in place

1.

Give as a gift to family or friends. Grandparents would love one.

We love you

Merry Christmas

Whatcha Need

Large white "flour sack" kitchen dish towel (approximately 22" x 38")
6' of satin ribbon, 1"–2" wide
White thread and needle (or an adult with a sewing machine)
Fabric paints (tube paints for writing names or words)
Paintbrushes

Whatcha Do

1. Hold the dish towel up to your shoulders. Have a friend mark the spot where the towel touches your knees. *(This will determine the length of the apron.)*
2. Fold the dish towel over at the mark. This is now the top of the apron.
3. Lay the ribbon down on the apron as shown in illustration 3.
4. Fold the top corners down, leaving 5" open at the center.
5. Sew the folded corners down in a triangle shape (illustration 4).
6. Adjust the ribbon loop so it fits over your head.
7. Sew the ribbon down at each corner to secure it (illustration 5).
8. Use the paintbrush to cover the palm of your hand with paint and make a handprint on the apron. Continue until you have made the design you want. Add words and details to the design using the fabric paint and brushes.

Option: Paint your thumbs and then make thumbprints!

Helping Hands Apron

© 1992 Concordia Publishing House

Sandpaper Sketch

Whatcha Need

Newspaper
Coarse sandpaper
Crayons
Drawing paper
Iron
Tagboard

Whatcha Do

1. Spread newspaper over your work area for easy clean-up after the project is finished.
2. Color large designs on the sandpaper with crayons. Be sure to press very hard as you work with the designs. (Remind the children that letters and numbers will come out backward.)
3. Place the sandpaper, colored side down, on the center of a piece of the drawing paper.
4. **Have an adult hold a hot iron over the back of the sandpaper until the crayon wax melts (approximately 10–15 seconds).**
5. Glue the outer edges of the picture onto a piece of tagboard as a backing.
6. To frame your "Sandpaper Sketch," see "Fun with Frames" (p. 23) or "Yarn Picture Frames" (p. 24).

© 1992 Concordia Publishing House

Witness Ball

Whatcha Need

Small "gifts" *
A package of crepe-paper streamers
Glue stick

Whatcha Do

1. Choose one of the gifts you have gathered and begin wrapping the crepe paper around it. Continue to wrap, making a ball and inserting additional gifts at various intervals as you wrap.
2. Use the glue stick to glue the end of the ball in place.
3. Give the ball to a friend. As your friend unwraps the gifts, explain the meaning behind each one.

   Gifts may also be made from dough recipes found in this book.

* Suggested gifts:

- A small cross to remind your friend that Jesus died and rose for us
- A heart to remind your friend that Jesus loves us
- A very small picture of Jesus
- Messages printed on quilling paper (e.g., "Jesus loves you" or "You are God's child") etc.
- Small wrapped candies

100

© 1992 Concordia Publishing House

Pillow Promises

Whatcha Need

Paper and pencils

Crayons

A white pillowcase (a solid, light color will also work)

Newspaper

Paper towels

Iron

Permanent felt-tipped marking pens *(optional)*

Whatcha Do

1. Create a design for your pillowcase. Draw it on paper first. Color it in.
2. Place several layers of newspaper inside the pillowcase and use crayons to color the design you have created, this time on the pillowcase. Remind children to press hard when using crayons.
3. Place a single layer of paper towels over the creation and then iron over it until all the wax melts out onto the paper towel. (An adult should do this!)
4. The picture will be permanently printed on the pillowcase. The case can be washed gently in warm water.

Note: For younger students, use large, block-style lettering to print a Bible promise and/or their names on their pillow cases. Then let them color in the letters and draw their own pictures with crayons.

Older children can design their own lettering and pictures using a combination of crayons and indelible marking pens.

Whatcha Need

Gelatin or cream cheese box
Glue
Yarn
Tongue depressor
Tape
Paper
Scissors
Pen

Whatcha Do

1. Cover one side of the box with glue. Arrange yarn in the glue in desired patterns. Fill the entire area.
2. Repeat this process on all sides of the box.
3. Open the bottom end of the box and tape one end of the tongue depressor to the inside.
4. Cut small pieces of contrasting color of yarn and glue it to all sides of the box (as "nuts" on the "ice cream bar").
5. Cut a strip of paper and print a message on it. Tape this to the tongue depressor. This message could be the Bible verse for the day or an invitation to VBS or the VBS closing worship service.

© 1992 Concordia Publishing House

Talent Box

Whatcha Need

One medium-size box (cereal box, shoebox, etc.)

Gift-wrapping paper

Cellophane tape

Ribbon or bow

Crayons or marking pens

Paper

Scissors

Glue

I can help.
I can serve.
I can sing.

My talents are Gifts from God.

Help the children identify the many talents and gifts God gives them.

Thank You, God
For voices that sing praises.
Thank You, God.
For hands that serve people.
Thank you, God
For ____
That ____
____
Thank You, God.

Whatcha Do

1. Wrap the box as a gift.
2. Discuss the talents God has given us. Ask the children to draw pictures of their talents on paper.
3. Cut out the pictures and glue them to the boxes.
4. Help the children to write a prayer of thanks.
5. Glue the prayer to the box.
6. Give your box a title, such as "My Talents Are a Gift from God."

© 1992 Concordia Publishing House

Theme Cross—
Bible Story Review

Whatcha Need
Seven plain tiles, each 3" square (found at a local tile store)
Acrylic paints
Paintbrush
One 12" wood slat
One 21" wood slat
Wood glue
A self-adhesive picture hanger

Whatcha Do

1. Paint a picture on each tile to depict a different Bible story (e.g., several Christmas narratives, the Passion/Easter accounts, stories you've studied lately in VBS or Sunday school). If necessary, fill in with Christian symbols so that each of the seven tiles is painted.
   (Note: Acrylic paint will not wash out of clothing. Wear old clothes or ask all students to wear paint shirts.)
2. Glue the short wood slat to the longer slat about 6" from one end to make a cross.
3. Glue each tile you painted onto the wooden slats.
4. Attach the picture hanger to the back of the cross near the top.

104

© 1992 Concordia Publishing House

Whatcha Need

Muslin, torn into 10 strips, each 1" x 4-1/2"; and 13 strips, each 1" x 13"
1" Styrofoam ball
Narrow ribbon cut in 3 pieces, each 8" long
Glue gun
Silver or gold pipe cleaner

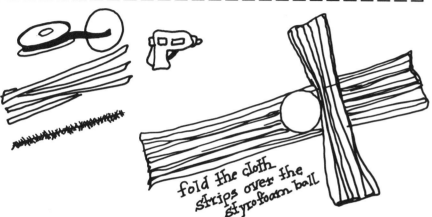

fold the cloth strips over the Styrofoam ball

Whatcha Do

1. Lay the long strips of muslin down side-by-side.
2. On top of these strips, about 5" from one end, lay the 4-1/2" strips perpendicular to the longer strips.
3. Place the Styrofoam ball (the angel's head) directly below the 4-1/2" strips.
4. Gently bring the ends of the 13" strips over the Styrofoam ball to make the angel's head. Make sure the ball is completely covered.
5. Use a piece of ribbon to tie these strips in place directly beneath the head and above the 4-1/2" strips, which have become the arms. Tie a knot, then a bow. Be sure to tie these strips tightly.
6. Tie a piece of ribbon directly beneath the arms. Tie a knot, then a bow.
7. Tie the third piece of ribbon in a knot to make a loop. Attach it to the back of the angel with a hot glue gun. **(An adult should use the hot glue gun.)**
8. Use half of the pipe cleaner (about 3") to form a halo. Glue the halo to the top of the angel's head.

© 1992 Concordia Publishing House

Cup Angels

Whatcha Need

A plastic or paper cup
X-Acto knife or safety-razor blade
A copy of the pattern on this page
Pencil
Scissors
Glitter, sequins, etc.
Hot glue gun
Thread

Whatcha Do

1. Before class an adult will need to cut out the bottom of the cup using an X-Acto knife or safety-razor blade. This will make the head of the angel.
2. Trace the pattern onto the cup.
3. Cut out the wings and arms.
4. Decorate the angel.
5. Cut a small triangle from the edge of the head.
6. An adult should use the hot glue gun to glue the head, wings, and arms in place.
7. Tie the thread to the cup between the wings and hang the angel from the ceiling, from a window latch, or Christmas tree.

God sends His angels to watch over us and to protect us.

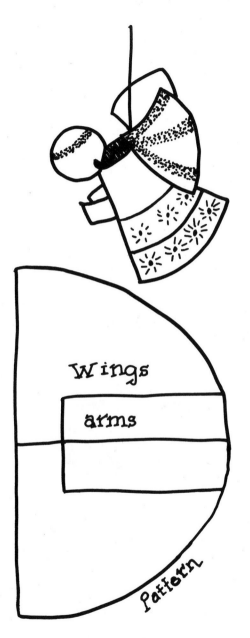

Wings

arms

Pattern

© 1992 Concordia Publishing House

PATTERN SHEETS

© 1992 Concordia Publishing House

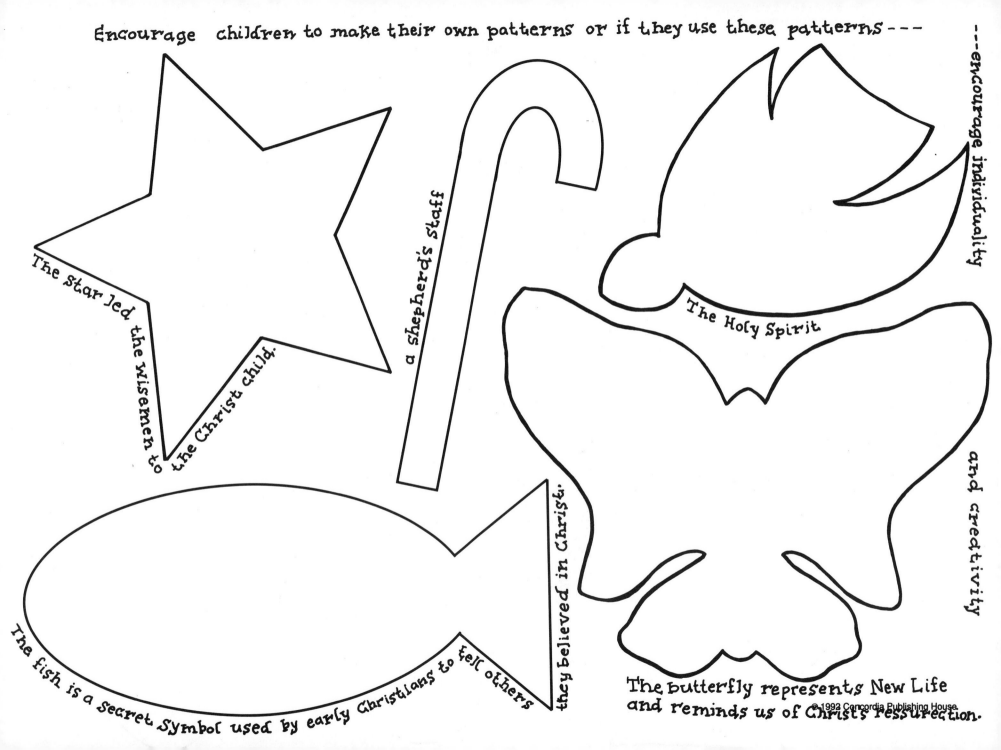

Encourage children to make their own patterns or if they use these patterns---

---encourage individuality

The star led the wisemen to the Christ child.

a shepherd's staff

The Holy Spirit

and creativity

The fish is a secret symbol used by early Christians to tell others they believed in Christ.

The butterfly represents New Life and reminds us of Christ's ressurection.

©1992 Concordia Publishing House

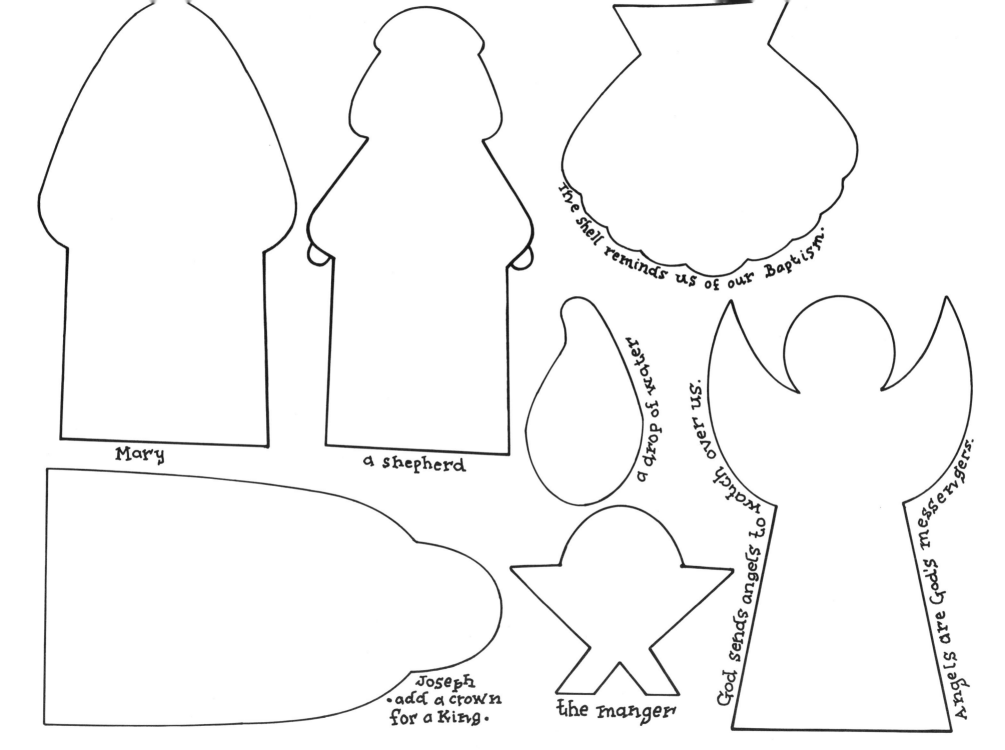

Mary

a shepherd

The shell reminds us of our Baptism.

a drop of water

Joseph
•add a crown
for a King.

the manger

God sends angels to watch over us.

Angels are God's messengers.

The ☧ is made up of the first two Greek letters of the word Christ.

New Life.

Christ is our anchor.

Christ, the King.

Notes

© 1992 Concordia Publishing House

Notes

© 1992 Concordia Publishing House